Adobe® LiveMotion™

fast&easy® web development

Katherine Murray

PRIMA TECH

A DIVISION OF PRIMA PUBLISHING

A Division of Prima Publishing

Prima Publishing and colophon are registered trademarks of Prima Communications, Inc. PRIMA TECH and Fast & Easy Web Development are registered trademarks of Prima Communications, Inc., Roseville, California 95661.

Publisher: Stacy L. Hiquet
Marketing Manager: Judi Taylor Wade
Associate Marketing Manager: Heather Buzzingham
Managing Editor: Sandy Doell
Acquisitions Editor: Debbie Abshier
Project Editor: Heather Talbot
Technical Reviewer: Keith A. Davenport
Copy Editor: Gabrielle Nemes
Interior Layout: Jill Flores
Cover Design: Prima Design Team
Indexer: Sharon Shock
Proofreader: Anne Owen

Adobe, the Adobe logo, Adobe GoLive, Adobe LiveMotion, and Adobe Photoshop are all trademarks or registered trademarks of Adobe Systems Incorporated.

Important: Prima Publishing cannot provide software support. Please contact the appropriate software manufacturer's technical support line or Web site for assistance.

Prima Publishing and the author have attempted throughout this book to distinguish proprietary trademarks from descriptive terms by following the capitalization style used by the manufacturer.

Information contained in this book has been obtained by Prima Publishing from sources believed to be reliable. However, because of the possibility of human or mechanical error by our sources, Prima Publishing, or others, the Publisher does not guarantee the accuracy, adequacy, or completeness of any information and is not responsible for any errors or omissions or the results obtained from use of such information. Readers should be particularly aware of the fact that the Internet is an ever-changing entity. Some facts may have changed since this book went to press.

ISBN: 0-7615-3254-4
Library of Congress Catalog Card Number: 00-109084
Printed in the United States of America

00 01 02 03 04 DD 10 9 8 7 6 5 4 3 2 1

Adobe®
LiveMotion™

fast&easy®
web development

Check the Web for Updates:

To check for updates or corrections relevant to this book and/or CD-ROM, visit our updates page on the Web at **http://www.prima-tech.com/updates**.

Send Us Your Comments:

To comment on this book or any other PRIMA TECH title, visit our reader response page on the Web at **http://www.prima-tech.com/comments**.

How to Order:

For information on quantity discounts, contact the publisher: Prima Publishing, P.O. Box 1260BK, Rocklin, CA 95677-1260; (916) 787-7000. On your letterhead, include information concerning the intended use of the books and the number of books you want to purchase.

Contents at a Glance

Contents

Acknowledgments

Designing for the Web and writing a book are similar processes in that neither can be done in a vacuum, thank goodness. I'd like to thank the terrific team at Prima for the time, energy, editorial talent, and direction they provided as we worked together to produce this book for you. Specifically, thanks to team leader Heather Talbot, Project Editor, for orchestrating people and pieces throughout this project; to Keith Davenport for a great and friendly technical edit; and to Gabrielle Nemes for her careful and conscientious editing. Finally, thanks to Debbie Abshier for being her wonderful acquisitional self, making sure everything goes smoothly for her authors. As always, I have enjoyed working with the Prima Tech team.

About the Author

Katherine Murray is the author of more than 40 books on a variety of topics, ranging from computer books (*Get Your Family on the Internet In a Weekend* and *Lotus Notes R5 Fast & Easy* Prima Tech, 1999), to business books (*Fundraising for Dummies*, IDG Books, 2000), to parenting books (*The Working Parents' Handbook: How to Succeed at Work, Maintain a Home, Raise Your Kids, and Still Have Time for You and Home but Not Alone: The Work-at-Home Parents' Handbook* Park Avenue Productions, 1998). She's also written many family and child-related articles for local and national magazines.

Katherine is a great believer in the possibility and potential of the Internet and loves researching and exploring new technologies as they develop. (Her children have given up telling her that she's a computer geek and are learning to live with having their own online time cut short so that Mom can do what she does.) Katherine has had her own business, reVisions Plus, Inc. (**http://www.revisionsplus.com**) for 13 years, offering writing and publishing support services to businesses and nonprofit organizations. She uses several Adobe products, including LiveMotion, as part of her services toolkit. You can reach Katherine at **kmurray@revisionsplus.com** or **kemurray@concentric.net**.

Introduction

Hello! and welcome to *Adobe LiveMotion Fast & Easy Web Development*, the newest offering in the *Fast & Easy Web Development* series from Prima Publishing. This book will help you learn the ins and outs of Adobe LiveMotion, one of the most exciting new Web graphics and animation programs available today. Whether you are new to Web graphics or are polishing up existing skills, you'll find helpful, to-the-point information here to help you create your visions as quickly as possible.

Who Should Read This Book?

The greatest thing about the *Fast & Easy Web Development* series is that it appeals to literally anyone wanting to learn more about Adobe LiveMotion. Because we focus on the steps you most need to know to learn the broadest number of the most-often-used features, you can use this book whether you're a Web guru or a brand-spanking-new beginner.

How to Get the Most from This Book

It's advice that works for life as well as for LiveMotion: Get what you need, use it, and move on. That's the basic concept behind the *Fast & Easy* series, as well. We don't give you a lot of fluff and hype about either the product or our book—we just want to give you what you need to enable you to start creating quickly. LiveMotion is a fun program, and once you have the basic how-tos, you can set your creative spirit loose to explore it fully on your own.

Each chapter in *Adobe LiveMotion Fast & Easy Web Development* teaches a specific area of LiveMotion, starting with the most basic procedures and leading to those that are more specialized. Each chapter includes sections that teach a specific task. And within each section, you will find illustrations and step-by-step instructions that show you—quickly and easily—how to master what you want to learn in LiveMotion.

In addition to this basic structure of the book, you will find elements that will help you learn more about LiveMotion as you go:

TIP

Tips give you extra information—hints and suggestions—for streamlining LiveMotion tasks.

NOTE

Notes provide a little more explanation, where necessary, about features and procedures covered in the steps.

Sidebars add some extra discussion about the task at hand, suggesting alternative methods or providing troubleshooting techniques.

At the end of this book, you'll find an appendix that walks you through the installation procedure, in case you need to install LiveMotion yourself. You'll also find a glossary for any unfamiliar terms you may find scattered through the text.

Get ready for your whirlwind tour—fast and easy!—through LiveMotion. And remember, LiveMotion is a hot new program just made for bringing life to the Web—so let your creative sparks fly!

1

Starting Out with LiveMotion

What are you in the mood to create? Do you have a great idea for a Web site, a slick animation with background music, or your company's new logo floating around in your head? This chapter introduces you to LiveMotion, a Web graphics and animation program from Adobe that can make all these ideas—and more—come to life. In this chapter, you'll learn how to

- See what LiveMotion can do.
- Install Adobe LiveMotion.
- Start LiveMotion and begin a new composition.
- Explore the LiveMotion work area.

What's Possible with LiveMotion?

Adobe has put together a great Web development package that includes Adobe GoLive, the Web generation program; Photoshop, which enables you to create customized photos and images; and Adobe Illustrator, one of the most popular drawing programs around. The animation piece of this package, and the newest member of the family, is LiveMotion. And although the other products in the Web development package complement what you can do with LiveMotion, you don't need to have the other products in order to create stunning Web graphics and animations on your own.

Create Web Interactivity and Motion

LiveMotion enables you to do all kinds of things that are related to movement, sound, and graphics on the Web. Here are a few ideas of things you may want to try:

• Create unique designs and illustrations.

• Use predesigned styles, textures, and library elements to create a professional look quickly.

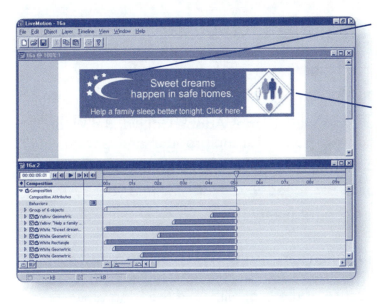

- Produce interactive Web features such as rollovers and pop-up elements.

- Develop Web videos, banner advertisements, and more.

Extend the Effectiveness of Your Work

Because it's easy to import files from and export files to Photoshop and GoLive, you can leverage the work you've done in those other programs, adding animation and interactive features easily.

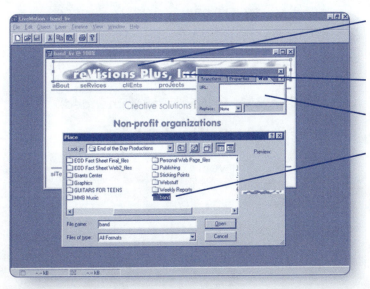

- Import an image you create in Photoshop.

- Turn it into a button.

- Add a Web link.

- Create a rollover so that it glows when the user points to it.

Installing LiveMotion

First things first. If you haven't yet installed LiveMotion, take a moment and do so now. Also check out the system requirements. It's better to know up–front what the program needs from your computer, because if your computer is overtaxed space– or speed–wise, you may find your system crashing frequently.

LiveMotion System Requirements

Because of the capabilities of the program, LiveMotion requires a hefty dose of system resources to run efficiently. Recommended system requirements are the following:

- Pentium II or faster (Windows).

  PowerPC or faster (Macintosh).

- Windows 98, NT SR4, or Windows 2000 (Windows).

  Mac OS 8.5 to 9.0 (Macintosh).

- 48MB of RAM (64MB is recommended).

- At least 100 MB of hard disk space.

- A CD–ROM drive.

NOTE

The newest version of LiveMotion, version 1.0.2, includes a number of enhancements and now works on Windows ME systems. If you are a Windows ME user and you have a previous version of LiveMotion, contact Adobe (www.adobe.com) to request the upgrade CD. If you use one of the other supported operating systems, you can download the upgrade directly from Adobe's Web site.

Beginning the Installation

LiveMotion may kick right into an auto–install process as soon as you put the CD–ROM in the drive. If so, follow the prompts on–screen to complete installation. If the installation process doesn't start on its own, you can install the program by following these steps:

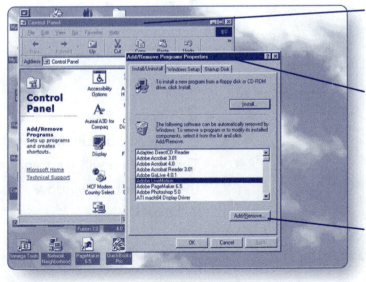

1. Open the Control Panel by choosing Start, Settings, Control Panel.

2. Double–click on Add/Remove Programs. The Add Remove Programs dialog box opens.

3. Insert the LiveMotion program CD–ROM in the CD–ROM drive; click on Install to start the process.

NOTE

The figures throughout this book were captured on a Windows 98 system, so some of the windows, dialog boxes, and options may appear somewhat differently than those you may see if you are using a Windows NT, 2000, or Macintosh system.

NOTE

Begin the installation process on the Mac by copying the LiveMotion installer file to your hard disk and then double–clicking its icon.

Starting LiveMotion

When you're ready to launch LiveMotion for the first time, follow these steps:

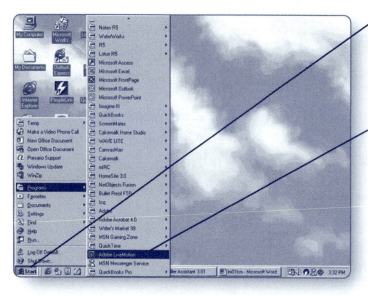

1. Click on the Start button in the Windows Taskbar. The Start menu will appear.

2. Click on Programs and choose Adobe LiveMotion. The program will start and the LiveMotion window will open.

Registering LiveMotion

The first time you start the program, the LiveMotion opening screen will appear. This screen gives you a number of links to resources, tips, tutorials, and more. Register your product (which makes you eligible for future updates and technical support) by clicking Register.

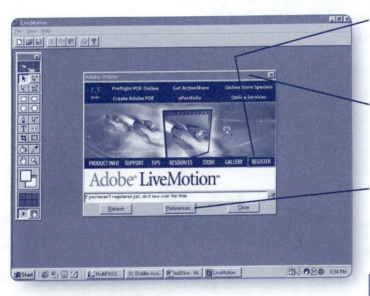

• Clicking on Register takes you online to the Adobe site.

• Get additional information about Adobe services.

• Set your preferences for how often you receive LiveMotion updates.

TIP

Redisplay the LiveMotion open screen later by clicking the topmost area of the Tools palette.

Setting Online Preferences

You can let Adobe know that you'd like to be in the queue to receive updates and information about

LiveMotion as it becomes available. Click on the Preferences button on the opening screen and then enter your user preferences, as follows:

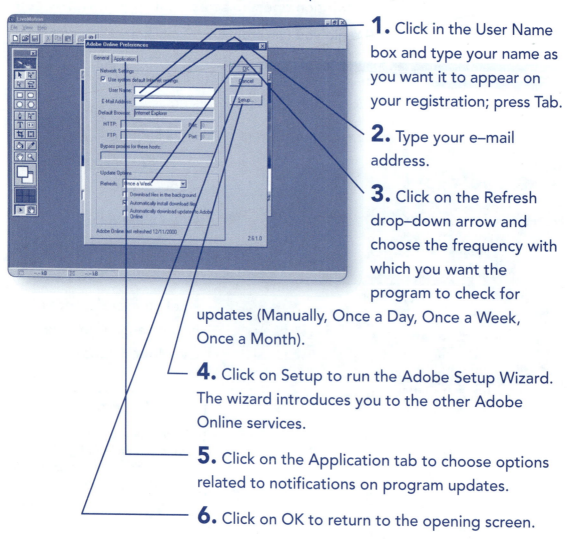

1. Click in the User Name box and type your name as you want it to appear on your registration; press Tab.

2. Type your e–mail address.

3. Click on the Refresh drop–down arrow and choose the frequency with which you want the program to check for updates (Manually, Once a Day, Once a Week, Once a Month).

4. Click on Setup to run the Adobe Setup Wizard. The wizard introduces you to the other Adobe Online services.

5. Click on the Application tab to choose options related to notifications on program updates.

6. Click on OK to return to the opening screen.

TIP

In Chapter 2, "Exploring the LiveMotion Workspace," you'll learn how to get help (both online and in the program) for any LiveMotion question you may have.

Starting a New Composition

When you start a new composition in LiveMotion, the program asks you to make a few choices about the file you will create.

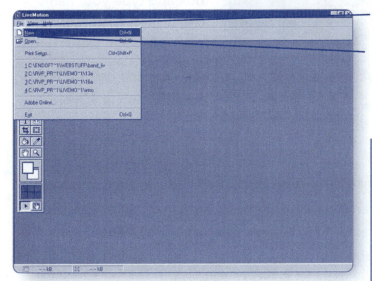

1. Choose File.

2. Choose New. The Composition Settings dialog box opens.

NOTE

When you first open LiveMotion, you may be greeted by several palettes. A palette in LiveMotion is a collection of options organized for a particular function. For example, the Colors palette enables you to choose colors for objects; the 3D palette sets 3–dimensional effects.

Choosing Composition Settings

When you first start a new composition, LiveMotion needs to know the size of the workspace, the way in which you want to export the file when you're finished, the frame rate, and whether you want to save the file in HTML format as well as in its native LiveMotion format.

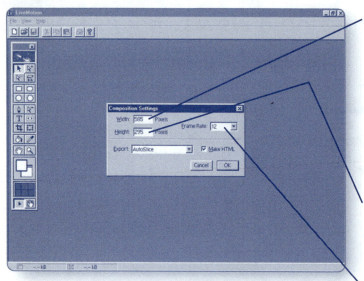

1. Type the width (in pixels) of the composition area you want to use. The width and height settings control the size of the area in which you will create your composition.

2. Type the height of the composition area you want.

3. Click on the Frame Rate drop–down arrow to choose the number of frames per second you want in an animation. The frame rate controls the number of frames per second displayed during an animation. The default setting is 12 frames per second.

TIP

You can change the Composition Settings at any time while you are working on a composition. You can easily change your settings later by opening the Edit menu and choosing Composition Settings.

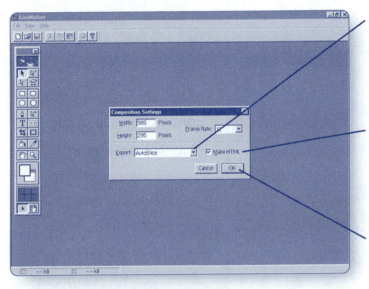

4. Click on the Export drop–down arrow to choose the export setting for the file.

5. Leave Make HTML selected to create an HTML file from the new composition.

6. Click on OK to create the new composition. The work area is created.

NOTE

You can export the compositions you create in LiveMotion so that you can use them with other programs. To learn more about LiveMotion's export features, see Chapter 18, "Exporting LiveMotion Creations."

Exploring the LiveMotion Workspace

The LiveMotion work area is a clean, easy–to–navigate space that gives you the tools you need to create the objects you want to animate. There are several key elements you will work with repeatedly:

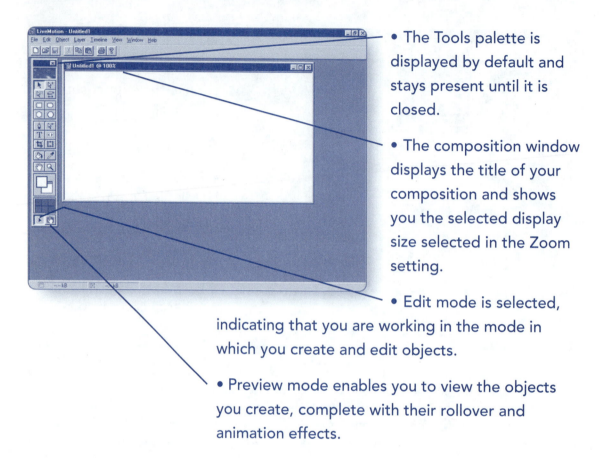

• The Tools palette is displayed by default and stays present until it is closed.

• The composition window displays the title of your composition and shows you the selected display size selected in the Zoom setting.

• Edit mode is selected, indicating that you are working in the mode in which you create and edit objects.

• Preview mode enables you to view the objects you create, complete with their rollover and animation effects.

NOTE

Chapter 2, "Exploring the LiveMotion Workspace," introduces you to the individual tools in the LiveMotion toolbox in the section, "Checking Out the Toolbox."

A Quick Summary

In this chapter, you learned about a few of the features offered by LiveMotion and how it can extend the reach of graphics you create in other programs, such as Photoshop and Illustrator.

Additionally, you discovered how to install and start the program and launch a new composition. In the next chapter, you learn to begin working with LiveMotion and find out how to get help when—and if—you need it.

2

Exploring the LiveMotion Workspace

Now that you've started LiveMotion and learned the basics of the composition area, you are ready for more in-depth exploring. In this chapter, you'll learn how to

- Use the LiveMotion menus.
- Check out the toolbox.
- Work with the Timeline.
- Get help with LiveMotion.

Using LiveMotion Menus

The LiveMotion menu bar, located at the top of the workspace, houses all the commands you need to create and work with graphics and animated objects in LiveMotion. The menus are the following:

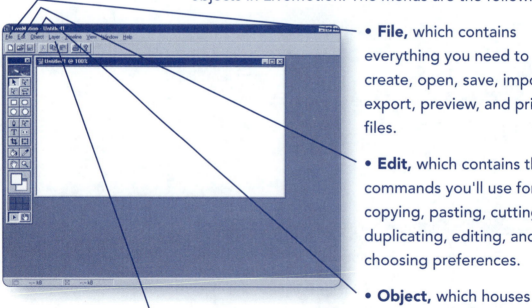

- **File,** which contains everything you need to create, open, save, import, export, preview, and print files.

- **Edit,** which contains the commands you'll use for copying, pasting, cutting, duplicating, editing, and choosing preferences.

- **Object,** which houses the commands for grouping and ungrouping, combining, arranging, converting, transforming, and distributing objects.

- **Layer,** which enables you to create, duplicate, delete, select, and arrange the layers in your objects.

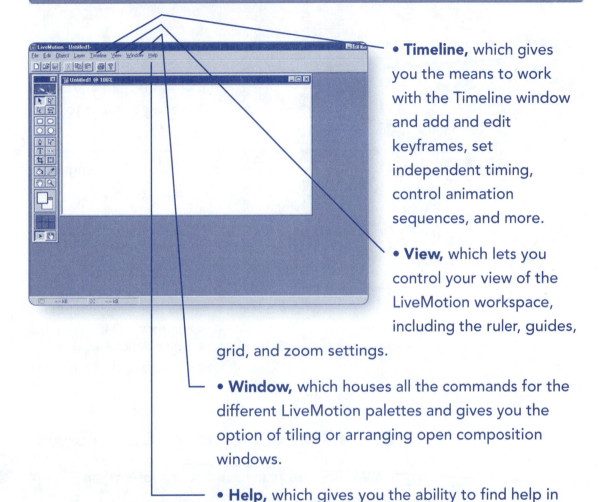

• **Timeline,** which gives you the means to work with the Timeline window and add and edit keyframes, set independent timing, control animation sequences, and more.

• **View,** which lets you control your view of the LiveMotion workspace, including the ruler, guides, grid, and zoom settings.

• **Window,** which houses all the commands for the different LiveMotion palettes and gives you the option of tiling or arranging open composition windows.

• **Help,** which gives you the ability to find help in the program or online.

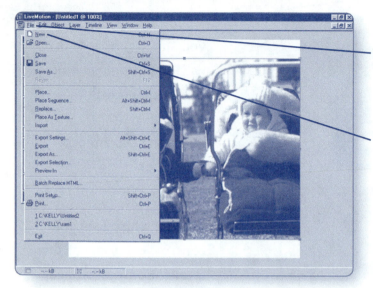

To open a menu, simply

1. Click on the name of the menu you want to open.

2. Click on the command you want to use.

TIP

You can optionally use the shortcut keys that appear to the right of most menu commands in lieu of opening the menus.

Displaying Submenus and Dialog Boxes

LiveMotion has many submenus, options, and dialog boxes nested within the primary menus.

To display a submenu and a dialog box:

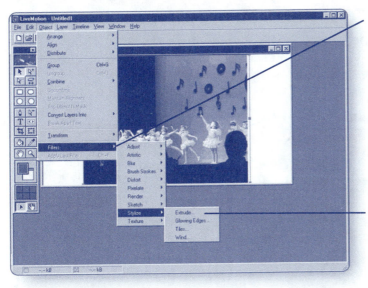

1. Point to a command that includes an arrow on the right. The command will be highlighted.

2. Click the mouse button. The submenu will appear.

3. Point to a command that has an ellipsis (...) to its right. The command will be highlighted.

4. Click the mouse button. A dialog box will open.

NOTE

One of the best ways to become familiar with the various features in LiveMotion is to open a file and begin experimenting with the many commands in the LiveMotion menus. Use something you can throw away later, but give yourself time to play around a bit. There are many great effects you may use in future projects that you might not have found had you not allowed yourself the time to explore.

Understanding LiveMotion Dialog Boxes

LiveMotion uses a number of dialog boxes to enable you to set controls and options for the objects you create. You will often find these features in LiveMotion dialog boxes:

• **Text boxes.** To enter a new value, click in the box and type the value you want.

• **Sliders.** These controls allow you to gradually change the selected setting. To change a slider value, drag the triangle in the direction of the change you desire.

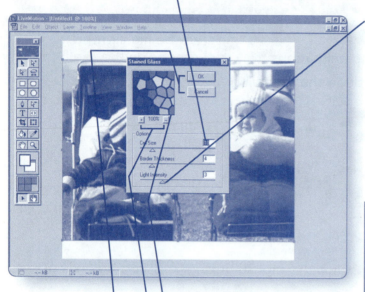

TIP
Press the Shift key while you drag the slider control to move the setting in increments of 10 units.

• **Preview window.** This window shows the effect of the change you make in the dialog box.

• **Increase and Decrease buttons.** Clicking either button changes the display of the preview window, allowing you to zoom in or out on the sample.

• **Command buttons.** Click on OK to accept your changes in the dialog box; click on Cancel or X to close the dialog box.

TIP
To exit a dialog box without making any changes, press Esc.

Checking Out the Toolbox

The LiveMotion toolbox includes the quick-access tools you'll need to create and work with graphics and animations. Key tool groups on the toolbox include the following:

• **Selection tools.** The four tools in this section—the Selection tool, the Subgroup Selection tool, the Drag Selection tool, and the Layer Offset tool—enable you to work with individual objects as well as with groups and layers of objects.

• **Shape tools.** The basic shape tools—Rectangle, Rounded Rectangle, Ellipse, and Polygon tools—let you create the basic shapes you need for the foundation of your custom drawings.

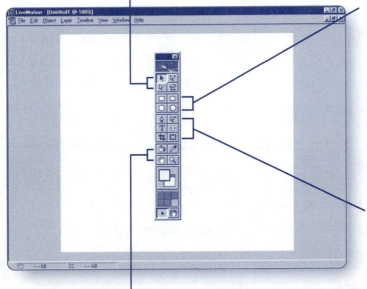

• **Drawing and editing tools.** These tools enable you to draw freehand (using the Pen tool), modify freehand objects (Pen Selection tool), enter text, add HTML tags, crop images, and transform or rotate an object.

• **Fill and view tools.** These tools allow you to control the color and pattern you use to fill an object, the way in which you pick up styles from other objects (Eyedropper tool), the placement of the object in the composition window (Hand tool), and the area of the composition you are viewing (Zoom tool).

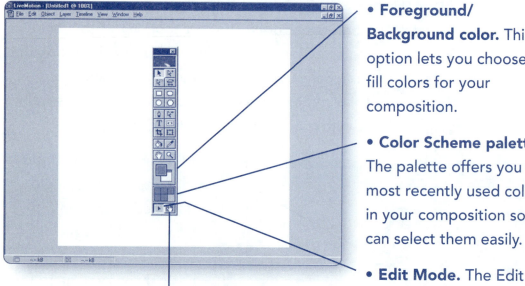

• **Foreground/ Background color.** This option lets you choose the fill colors for your composition.

• **Color Scheme palette.** The palette offers you the most recently used colors in your composition so you can select them easily.

• **Edit Mode.** The Edit Mode button lets you switch easily into edit mode after you have previewed an animation.

• **Preview Mode.** The Preview Mode button enables you to run through a preview of an animation you have created.

TIP

You can learn the individual names of each tool by positioning the mouse pointer over the tool. The name of the tool will appear in a ToolTip over the tool, telling you the tool's name.

TABLE 2.1 Toolbox Shortcut Keys

To select this tool	Press this (Macintosh and Windows)
Selection	V
Subgroup Selection	A
Drag Selection	U
Layer Offset	O
Rectangle	M
Rounded Rectangle	R
Ellipse	L
Polygon	N
Pen	P
Pen Selection	S
Type	T
HTML Text	Y
Crop	C
Transform	E
Paint Bucket	K
Eyedropper	I
Hand	H
Zoom	Z
Edit Mode/Preview Mode	Q

Hiding and Redisplaying the Toolbox

When you first start LiveMotion, the toolbox is automatically displayed on the screen. If you want to hide the toolbox to make more room on-screen and then redisplay it later, you can do so easily by following these steps:

1. Click on Window. The Window menu will appear.

2. Click on Tools. The Toolbox will be hidden.

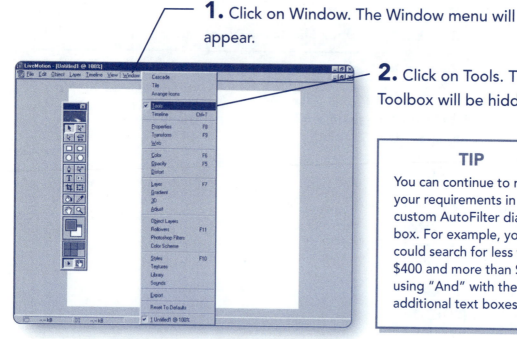

TIP

You can continue to refine your requirements in the custom AutoFilter dialog box. For example, you could search for less than $400 and more than $350 using "And" with the additional text boxes.

Exploring the Timeline

The LiveMotion Timeline looks like it's all about orchestrating animated objects. And that is the job of the Timeline—to give you the means to sequence the animation of the objects you create in LiveMotion. However, you can also work with groups of objects by selecting them and ordering them in the Timeline. Some things you'll do using the Timeline window include the following:

- Animating objects.
- Controlling the way objects behave.

- Setting the duration of animations.

- Selecting and working with groups of objects.

NOTE

For in-depth information on the specifics of using the Timeline, see Chapter 14, "Working with the LiveMotion Timeline."

Displaying the Timeline

The Timeline window looks very different from the LiveMotion composition window. Each object in your animation is listed in the Timeline, along with the various properties you have selected for those objects. All this comes into play when you're ready to animate your creations.

To display the Timeline:

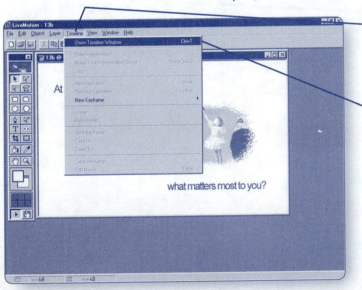

1. Click on the Timeline menu name. The Timeline menu will appear.

2. Click on Show Timeline Window. The Timeline window will then be displayed.

TIP

You can also use shortcut keys to display the Timeline. Press Ctrl+T if you are using Windows or Cmd+T if you are using the Mac. The shortcut keys also work as a toggle, which means you can hide the Timeline window by repeating the keystrokes.

Tiling the Display

The easiest way to work with both the Timeline and the composition windows is to tile them so they are both visible at the same time.

• Open the Window menu and choose Tile. Both the composition window and the Timeline will be visible on your screen.

• Resize or move the windows as needed to create maximum workspace.

NOTE

If you have other compositions open when you choose Tile, those files will be displayed, too. Be sure to close unnecessary files before you tile the display; otherwise, you'll have to close the windows manually.

Reviewing the Timeline Window

A quick scan of the Timeline window shows you the important elements in the Timeline:

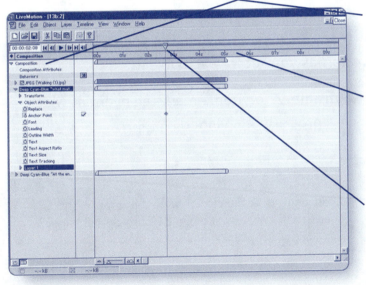

• **Objects column.** Choose the object with which you want to work here.

• **Timeline.** The metered time segments enable you to see the animation playing over time.

• **Current Time Marker.** This marker shows where the animation is at a precise moment.

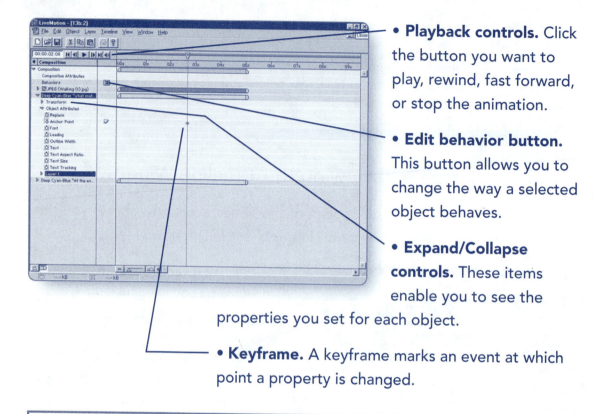

• **Playback controls.** Click the button you want to play, rewind, fast forward, or stop the animation.

• **Edit behavior button.** This button allows you to change the way a selected object behaves.

• **Expand/Collapse controls.** These items enable you to see the properties you set for each object.

• **Keyframe.** A keyframe marks an event at which point a property is changed.

TIP

When you are ready to put the Timeline away, click the close box in the upper-right corner of the Timeline window or press Ctrl+T (Windows) or Cmd+T (Macintosh) again.

Getting LiveMotion Help

Although LiveMotion is fairly intuitive to use, especially if you are familiar with the other Adobe products such as Photoshop, there will be a number of new phrases and concepts that may be new to you. To get help and/or ideas for specific ways to use tools and techniques, you can consult LiveMotion Help.

Using Program Help

To display Help within the LiveMotion program, follow these steps:

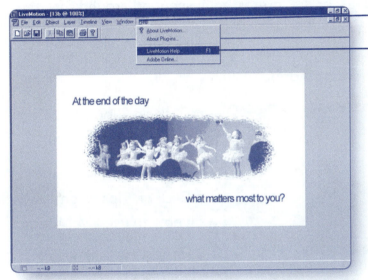

1. Click the Help menu.

2. Choose LiveMotion Help or press F1. The Help window appears in your browser interface.

You have three choices for the way in which you get help from LiveMotion:

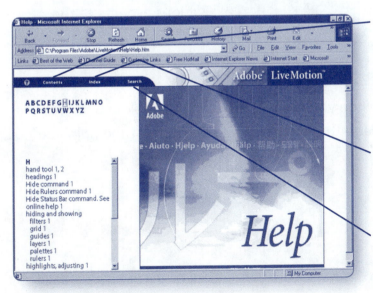

• You can read the basics of working with the program by clicking Contents and selecting your topic.

• Click on Index and select the letter of the topic you want to look up.

• Click on Search and enter the word or phrase about which you want to find out more information.

Accessing Online Help

Adobe offers a number of different resources online for those times when you need help, want ideas, or are interested in scouting around for other services that will help you in your work. You can access online help by opening the Help menu and choosing Adobe Online.

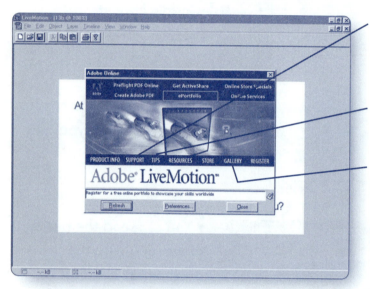

• Click on Support to access online technical support.

• Click on Tips to get ideas on how to use LiveMotion.

• Click in Gallery to see sample tutorials on the various aspects of the program.

When you click Support, you are taken to a Web page that enables you to search for the help you need.

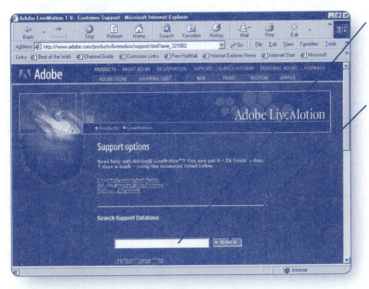

1. Enter the word or phrase for which you want to search.

2. Click on Search. After a moment, the research results will be shown in the form of links to knowledge base articles that include questions and answers from LiveMotion users and Adobe technical support staff.

A Quick Summary

This chapter has introduced you to the tools on the LiveMotion workspace, briefed you on the Timeline, and showed you how to access in-program and online help. The next chapter walks you through the palettes you will work with while setting properties for the LiveMotion objects you create.

3

A LiveMotion QuickStart

Before diving right in and learning to create, enhance, and animate objects in LiveMotion, it's a good idea to get a sense of the overall process. This chapter takes you through all of the steps involved in animating a simple object. You'll learn specifically how to

- Create a basic object.
- Enhance the object by adding a style.
- Apply a rollover effect to the object.
- Animate an object with preset animation.
- Create an object link to a Web page.
- Export the object.

NOTE

In LiveMotion, an object is the basic element you create, modify, move, and change as part of your animation sequence. For more about creating and working with LiveMotion objects, see Chapter 5, "Adding and Importing Objects."

Creating Basic Objects

LiveMotion objects are the basic building blocks on which everything in the program is based. Four different types of objects are available:

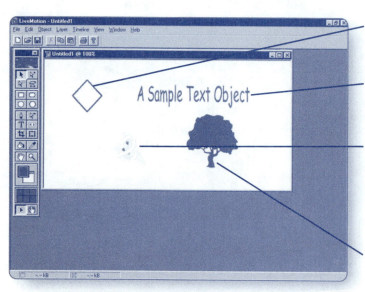

- Shapes created with the drawing tools.

- Text added using the Text tool.

- Paint graphics (bitmapped) imported from another program (such as Photoshop).

- Draw graphics (vector) imported from another program (such as Illustrator).

NOTE

Vector graphics are based on calculations, which means you can enlarge or reduce them without any loss of clarity. Bitmap graphics are graphics that are actually a *map of bits*, or a pattern of individual pixels.

Creating a Shape

Start by creating a simple shape. If you haven't already done so, start a new composition. (If you need to review the steps for starting a new file, see Chapter 1, "Starting Out with LiveMotion.")

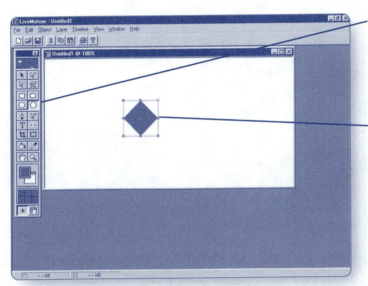

1. Click on the tool you want to use and move the mouse pointer to the workspace.

2. Drag the mouse pointer to draw the shape. You can resize or rotate the shape as desired by dragging the handles on the sides or corner of the object.

NOTE

The color of your object is determined by the color preselected in the foreground in the Toolbox. Chapter 9, "Selecting Colors for Compositions," explains how to work with color in LiveMotion.

Enhancing Objects by Choosing a Style

Next, you can add a professional touch to the object by adding a style. A *style* is a ready-made set of attributes that give an object a certain look and feel. You might use a style, for example, to turn an object into a 3D button, add a highlight, assign a specific color, and even add a rollover effect. Here are the steps for adding a style to an object:

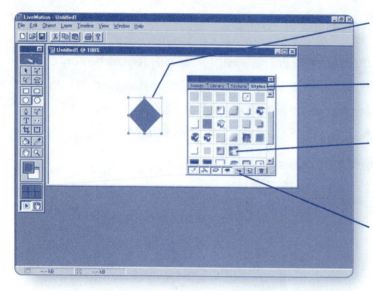

1. Select the object, if necessary.

2. Open the Styles palette by pressing F10.

3. Click on the icon for the style you want to apply to the object.

4. Click on the Apply Style button. The style is added to the selected object.

Adding Interactivity with Rollover Effects

You can see how easy it is to make even simple creations look good. The next step involves adding some interactivity to the object you're developing. A *rollover effect* is a movement or change to the object that occurs when the user performs a mouse action such as clicking, pointing, or moving the pointer off an object.

You can easily add a rollover effect to your object using these steps:

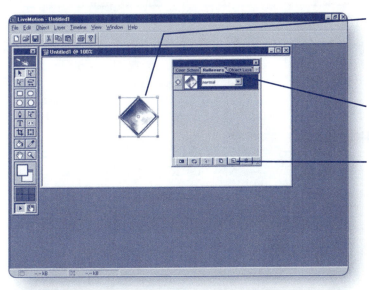

1. Verify that the object is selected. (Handles appear around a selected object.)

2. Open the Rollover palette by pressing F11.

3. Click on the New Rollover State button. A new line is added to the Rollover palette.

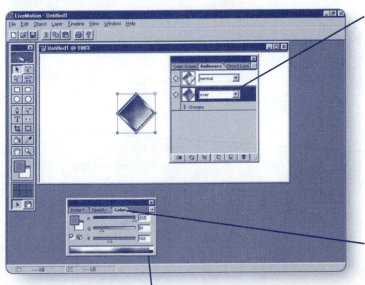

4. Click on the Rollover state drop-down arrow and choose Over, if it isn't automatically selected. This creates a new rollover state that will respond when the user positions the mouse pointer over the object.

5. Press F6 to open the Color palette, if necessary. This enables you to change the color so that a new color displays when the user moves the pointer over the object.

6. Click on the color you want to assign to the new rollover state.

NOTE

Color is just one example of a change you can make in a rollover. You can also play a sound, change styles, create a *glow*, or cause a remote image to appear. These different rollover possibilities are explored in Chapter 13, "Creating Rollover Techniques."

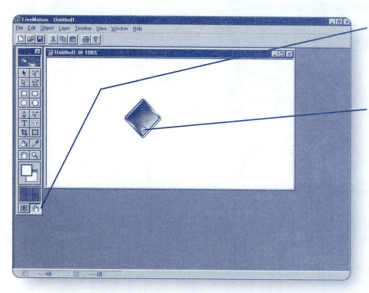

7. Preview the rollover by clicking on the Preview Mode button.

8. Move the mouse pointer to the object to see the effect of the rollover.

TIP

Adding a sound effect to a rollover, such as key click, is also a simple matter. For more about adding sound effects to your compositions, see Chapter 16, "Sounding Off with Sound Objects."

Animating Objects

Although animation is often thought to be a long elaborate sequence in which many different actions take place, an animation can be as simple as rotating an object a few points in a single direction. Animation can also be as simple as one color fading into the next or text jiggling around on-screen.

The LiveMotion Library includes several preset animations that you can apply to the objects you create. To use one of these preset animations, follow these steps:

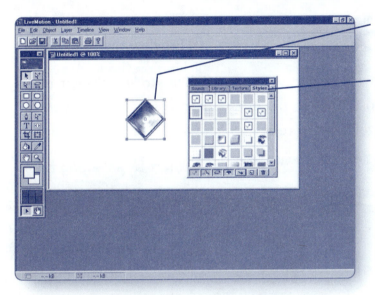

1. Verify that your object is selected.

2. Open the Styles palette by pressing F10, if necessary.

3. Verify that only the View Styles with Animation button is selected. (Click the other buttons to deselect them.) Only the styles with animations are displayed.

4. Click on the Animation style you want.

5. Click on the Apply Style button. The style is applied to the object.

6. Click on the Preview Mode button to preview the animation.

NOTE

Creating animations that are more elaborate involves the use of the Timeline, which you learn about in Chapter 14, "Working with the LiveMotion Timeline."

Creating Web Links

LiveMotion gives you the ability to link objects of all sorts to Web pages or other files on your server or Web site. Here are the steps to create a quick link:

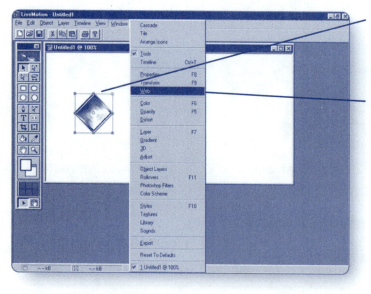

1. Start by selecting the object to which you want to apply the link.

2. Open the Web palette by choosing Web from the Window menu.

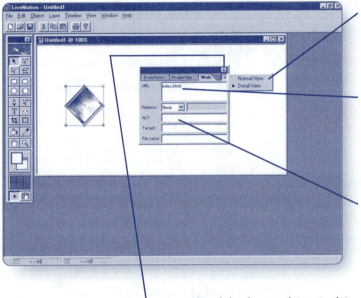

3. Click on the view selector arrow and choose Detail view.

4. Type the URL for the Web page or the filename to which you want to link the object.

5. Type a description for the object, if necessary. (This alternate text will appear only if the user has disabled graphics in his or her browser preferences.)

6. When finished, click on the Web palette's close box.

Exporting Compositions

The final step in preparing your LiveMotion object for the Web is exporting the file to a format that can be used in other programs. You might want to export the file simply to an HTML file, or you might want to use the object you create in a Web page generator like GoLive.

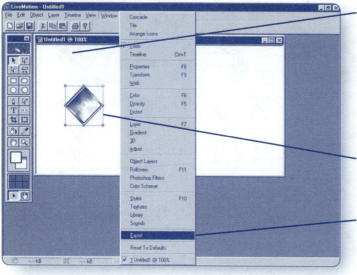

1a. If you want to explore an entire composition, verify that no objects are selected.

OR

1b. If you want to export a specific object, select it.

2. Click on the Window menu and choose Export to open the Export palette.

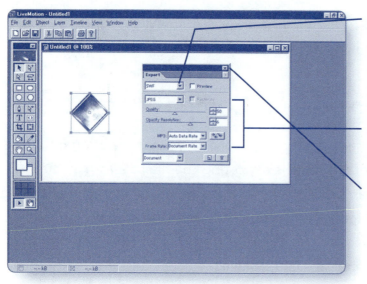

3. Choose the format to which you want to export the file. (SWF is the Flash format.)

4. Select the various export settings as needed.

5. Click on the close box to close the palette.

NOTE

You can export LiveMotion objects and compositions to a number of different formats, including SWF, JPEG, GIF, and PNG. For more about exporting LiveMotion files, see Chapter 18, "Exporting LiveMotion Creations."

Exporting a Selected Object

If you want to export only a single object or a group of objects in your composition, you can do so using the Export Selection dialog box. Begin by selecting the object you want to export. If you want to export a group of objects, select the items and open the Objects menu and choose Group. Then follow these steps:

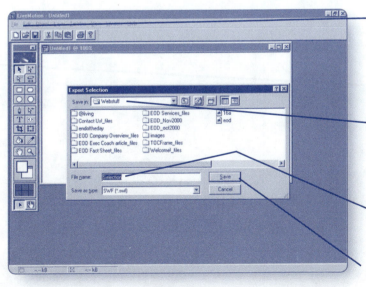

1. From the File menu, choose Export (in this example, Export Selection was chosen).

2. Choose the folder in which you want to save the exported file.

3. Type a filename for the file.

4. Click on Save to complete the export.

A Quick Summary

This chapter has introduced you to all the basic procedures in putting together a LiveMotion animation. As you go along, you'll learn to add and customize colors and styles and create your own special effects. The next chapter shows you how to customize your LiveMotion workspace.

4

Customizing the LiveMotion Workspace

A comfortable workspace is a productive workspace. This chapter focuses on ways in which you might want to change or re-arrange the composition (or workspace) area to your liking. In this chapter, you will learn to

- Open and close palettes.
- Add rulers.
- Control grids and guides.
- Set LiveMotion preferences.

Opening Palettes

Palettes are movable boxes containing options for various features. Palettes can be positioned anywhere on the screen while you work, and can be opened and closed at will. If you need to change a color, for example, you can open the palette briefly and then put it away again (close it) until it is needed again. There's no need to have palettes continually open on your composition area, cluttering your workspace. To open a palette, follow these steps:

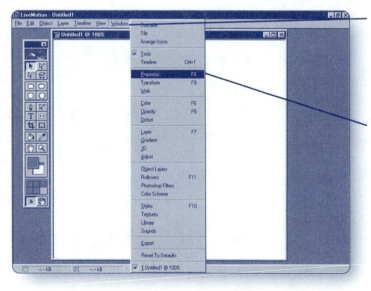

1. Begin with an open file. Click on the Window menu. The Window menu appears.

2. Click on the name of the palette you want to open. The palette opens on the screen. Table 4.1 spotlights the most commonly used palettes and lists the shortcut keys used to open them.

TABLE 4.1 LiveMotion Palettes

Palette	Description	Shortcut Key (Win)	Shortcut Key (Mac)
Color	Choose and change colors	F6	F6
Export	Enter settings for file export to HTML or other formats	Ctrl+Alt+Shift+E	Cmd+Opt+Shift+E
Layers	Select current layer or copy, delete, or move layers	F7	F7
Opacity	Control the opacity of the selected object or layer	F5	F5
Properties	Select settings for the selected object	F8	F8
Rollovers	Add, change, or remove a rollover effect for the selected object	F11	F11
Styles	Choose a style to apply to the selected object	F10	F10
Collapse outline to hide text		Alt+Shift+minus sign	

Each of the LiveMotion palettes is used similarly:

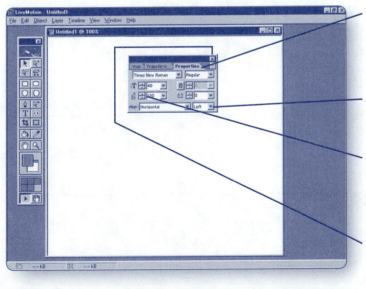

• Click a tab to work with different groups of options.

• Click a drop-down arrow to display a submenu.

• Click the Increase or Decrease button to change the entered value.

• Click the close box to close the palette.

Splitting Palettes

You can also create your own palette by splitting off a tab you use often. Follow these steps:

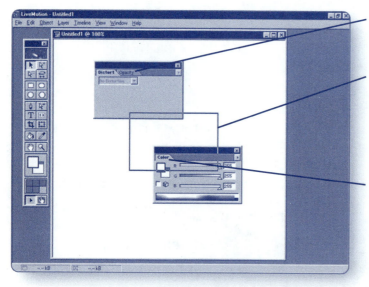

1. Point to the tab you want to move.

2. Drag the tab to a new location on the screen. The outline of the tab will move with the pointer.

3. Release the mouse button. The tab is displayed in a new palette in the LiveMotion workspace.

Closing Palettes

You can close a palette using three different methods:

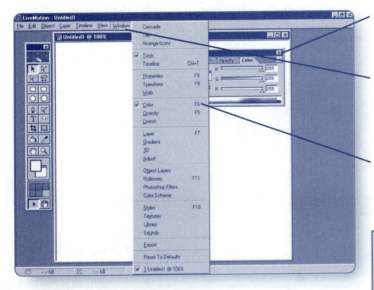

• Click on the palette close box.

• From the Window menu, choose the palette name to close.

• Press the function key assigned to the palette.

Adding Rulers

Does your current project require that you create an object according to certain specifications? If you're dealing with precise measurements, you'll need the LiveMotion ruler. To display the rulers, use these steps:

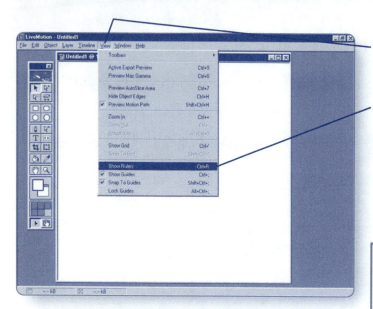

1. Click on View. The View menu will appear.

2. Click on Show Rulers. Rulers will be displayed along the left and top sides of the composition area.

NOTE

Do the numbers on the ruler look odd? Those are pixels, not the picas or inches you might be familiar with.

TIP

You can display and hide the rulers with a single keystroke by pressing Ctrl+R in Windows or Cmd+R on the Mac.

Working with Grids and Guides

Grids and guides give you additional ways to control the objects you create in LiveMotion. To display the grid, follow these steps:

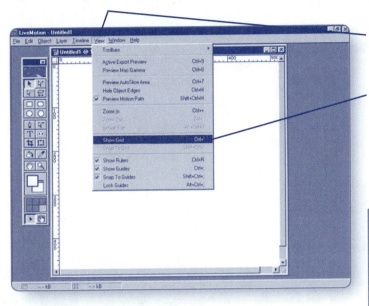

1. Click on View. The View menu will appear.

2. Click on Show Grid. A grid of blue lines will appear in the composition area.

NOTE

The Grid is a mesh of horizontal and vertical guides that help you create your objects according to linear boundaries. The Grid will not print when you print your LiveMotion compositions.

TIP

You can continue to refine your requirements in the custom AutoFilter dialog box. For example, you could search for less than $400 and more than $350 using "And" with the additional text boxes.

Adding Guides

Once you begin working with objects in LiveMotion, you will find that guides are helpful for aligning the various elements in your composition. You can add guides easily:

NOTE

Guides are nonprinting lines that appear over your objects as you work with them. They help you ensure that different parts of your object align.

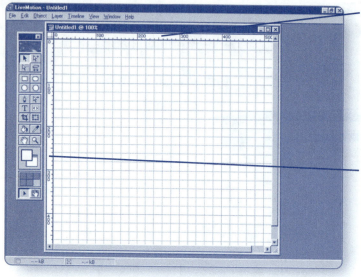

• To create a horizontal guide, click in the horizontal ruler and drag the pointer to the place in the workspace where you want to set the guide.

• To create a vertical guide, click in the vertical ruler and drag the pointer to the place you want to establish the vertical guide.

TIP

If you want to suppress the display of guides, click on View and choose Show Guides.

To move guides on the LiveMotion workspace, simply drag them to the new location.

To delete a guide, hold Ctrl (Windows users) or Cmd (Mac users) while dragging the guide back to the ruler.

Setting LiveMotion Preferences

LiveMotion lets you control a few of the basic settings on which you'll rely as you interact with the program. In the Preferences dialog box, you choose whether the Arrow tool is selected automatically, how large or small you want the grid to be, and whether or not the Windows system font is used (if you're using the PC version of LiveMotion).

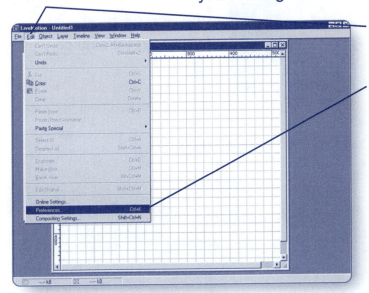

1. Click on Edit. The Edit menu will appear.

2. Click on Preferences. The Preferences dialog box will open.

TIP

You can continue to refine your requirements in the custom AutoFilter dialog box. For example, you could search for less than $400 and more than $350 using "And" with the additional text boxes.

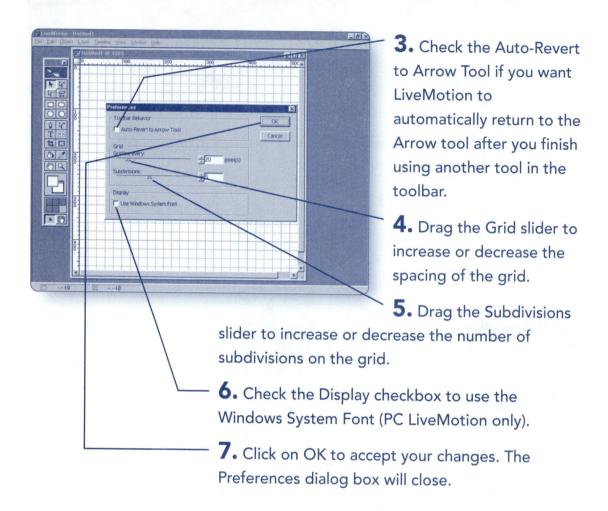

3. Check the Auto-Revert to Arrow Tool if you want LiveMotion to automatically return to the Arrow tool after you finish using another tool in the toolbar.

4. Drag the Grid slider to increase or decrease the spacing of the grid.

5. Drag the Subdivisions slider to increase or decrease the number of subdivisions on the grid.

6. Check the Display checkbox to use the Windows System Font (PC LiveMotion only).

7. Click on OK to accept your changes. The Preferences dialog box will close.

NOTE

On the Mac, you will see another option in the Preferences dialog box: Append File Extension. This option tells LiveMotion to add its file extension to the end of the filenames you create in LiveMotion. This makes transferring files between PCs and Macs easier.

A Quick Summary

This chapter showed you how to set up your workspace the way you want it. You learned how to open and close the various palettes, along with how to add rulers, grids, and guides. Finally, you found out about the LiveMotion preferences that give you further control to the LiveMotion display. The next chapter steps into the composition area by showing you how to draw simple shapes and how to place art from other programs.

5

Adding and Importing Objects

Are you eager to get busy creating objects? This chapter helps you create new LiveMotion objects by drawing, importing, or placing them in a composition. In this chapter, you will learn how to

- Use the drawing tools to create objects.
- Import objects you've created in other programs.
- Place existing objects in your composition.

Using the Drawing Tools to Create Objects

LiveMotion includes a set of drawing tools you can use to create your own objects. If you've ever used a drawing program before, you'll find your way around in no time.

Displaying the Grid

If you're like me, drawing by hand isn't your strong suit. You can display the grid to help guide your shape creations. Here's how:

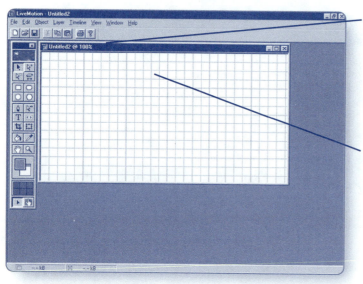

1. Create a new composition. (If you need to review the steps, see Chapter 1, "Starting Out with LiveMotion.")

2. Click on View and choose Show Grid. The grid appears in your new workspace.

Adding the Snap to the Grid

Having the grid available as a visual guide may be all the help you need, but some of us need extra guidance. If you want to make the grid "sticky" so that the items you draw by hand "snap" to the gridlines, follow these steps:

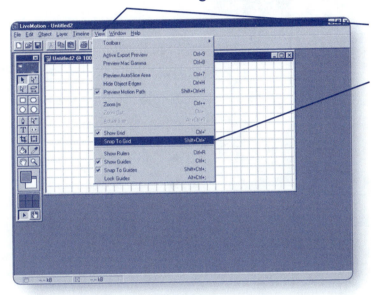

1. Open the View menu again.

2. Click on Snap to Grid.

Reviewing the Drawing Tools

Now that you have a space to work in, you can begin creating simple shapes. LiveMotion gives you a familiar set of drawing tools:

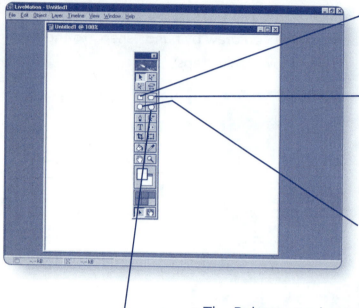

• The Rectangle tool lets you draw squares and rectangles.

• The Rounded Rectangle tool gives you the option of drawing squares and rectangles with rounded (or curved) corners.

• The Ellipse tool makes it possible to draw circles and ovals.

• The Polygon tool gives you the means to draw multi-sided shapes made of straight lines.

Drawing an Object

Depending on the object you want to draw and the tool you choose to use, drawing can be very simple. Whether you want to create a shape, a curve, or a shadow layer for a multi-layer object, the process of using the tool is the same:

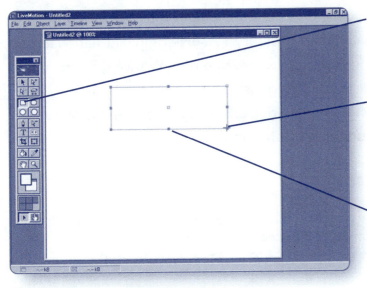

1. Click on the rectangle tool. The mouse pointer changes to a crosshair.

2. Drag the crosshair in any direction you choose. A box will be drawn on the screen.

3. Release the mouse button. The rectangle appears with handles along the edges.

TIP

If you don't like the look of things, you can easily delete what you've just drawn by selecting the object and pressing Del. You can also open the Edit menu and choose Undo.

Importing Objects

Another way to get art objects into LiveMotion includes importing them. *Importing* in LiveMotion is really about scanning images or bringing them in from another digital source (such as a digital camera or audio or video recorder).

If you want to import images into LiveMotion, install the necessary TWAIN-compliant hardware and software before you begin. Adobe offers a number of plug-ins (available on the Web at **http://www.adobe.com**) that you can install to work with LiveMotion.

NOTE

What's TWAIN? No, not a country singer or the caustic creator of *Huckleberry Finn*. It's a standard for equipment that produces digitized files. You'll see the term *TWAIN-compliant* to refer to an industry standard scanning device or other digital tool.

To import an image into LiveMotion, use these steps:

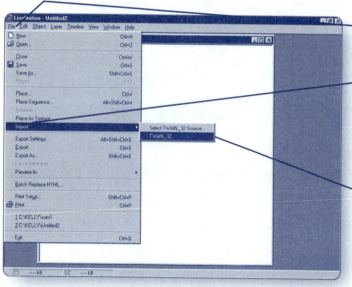

1. Click on File. The File menu will appear.

2. Click on Import. A submenu will appear, listing your TWAIN source choices.

3. Click on TWAIN_32. After a moment, the dialog box for your particular scanner will open.

NOTE

If you have not set up your scanner or digital camera to work with LiveMotion, use the option Select TWAIN_32 Source to do so before you select TWAIN_32 from the Import submenu. This is also important to do if you are switching between imaging devices, such as a digital camera and a scanner.

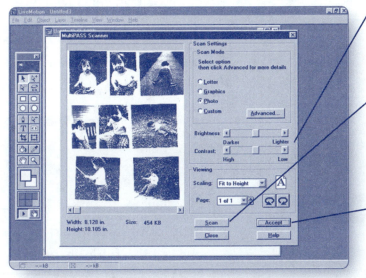

4. Choose the options that are appropriate for your scanner.

5. Click on Scan. The scanner will scan the document and display it in the preview box.

6. Make any changes you need and repeat, or click Accept. The image will then be placed as a bitmap object in your LiveMotion composition.

NOTE

Are you wondering about the difference between vector and bitmap graphics? Vector graphics are those that are drawn based on calculations, which means you can enlarge or reduce them without any loss of clarity. Bitmap graphics are graphics that are actually a *map of bits*, or a pattern of individual pixels. When you enlarge a bitmap graphic, the pixels are larger and more visible, resulting in a loss of quality. LiveMotion enables you to import and place both vector and bitmap graphics.

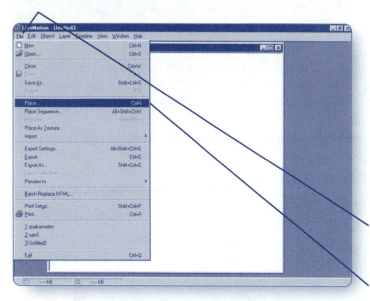

Placing Objects

The final way you can get LiveMotion objects into your composition involves placing them in the composition window. Here is the process:

1. Click on File. The File menu will appear.

2. Click on Place. The Place dialog box will open.

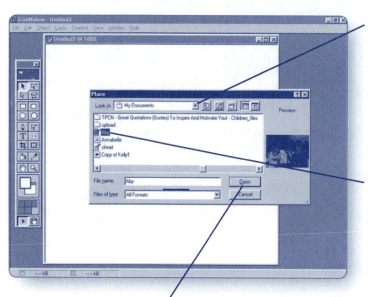

3. Click on the Look in drop-down arrow and choose the folder in which the image you want to place is stored. The file list will show your choices.

4. Click on the file you want to use. A preview of the file will appear in the Preview area of the dialog box.

5. Click on Open to open the file. The image will be placed in the composition window.

TIP

LiveMotion can handle files in all these different file formats: BMP (Windows), EPS, GIF, JPEG, PICT (Mac), PNG, and TIFF.

TIP

LiveMotion also enables you to place a group of files you've created in Photoshop or Illustrator as a *sequence*, which turns them into a single LiveMotion animation. You simply create the individual files in Photoshop or Illustrator, naming them sequentially (such as flight01.psd, flight02.psd, and so on). Then, in LiveMotion, choose File and Place Sequence to place the files.

A Quick Summary

This chapter has shown you how to get objects into your LiveMotion compositions. You learned how to draw objects using LiveMotion's drawing tools, import objects via your scanner, and place graphics files you've created in other programs. The next chapter shows you how to do some simple editing and arranging of the objects you've created.

6

Editing and Transforming Objects

One of the coolest things about working with Web graphics and animation is that you can take something that starts in a simple form—a photo of the dog, a video clip of a school play—and turn it into something else that adds just the right touch to the story you're telling. This chapter shows you how to work with the objects you have created in your LiveMotion composition. In this chapter, you'll learn how to

- Select objects.
- Duplicate objects.
- Align objects.
- Move, resize, and crop objects.
- Group and ungroup objects.
- Transform objects.
- Make simple modifications.
- Delete objects.

> **NOTE**
>
> What counts as an object in LiveMotion? As you learned in Chapter 5, "Adding and Importing Objects," you can open other LiveMotion files, import clip art, picture files, animation files, scanned photos, and art you draw. You can also add sound objects as part of your LiveMotion composition.

Selecting Objects

Selecting objects is a simple task and LiveMotion provides you with three separate selection tools. To select an object or a group of objects, you must first click one of these tools:

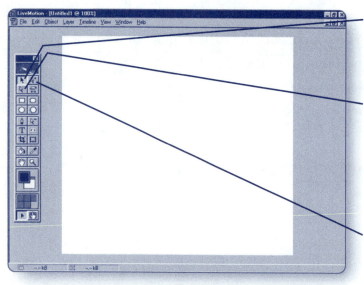

• **Selection Tool.** Use this tool to select a single object.

• **Drag Selection Tool.** Click this tool to drag a mouse pointer over layered objects that you want to select.

• **Subgroup Selection Tool.** Click this tool to select either a subgroup or an individual object that is part of a group.

TIP

Don't forget the quick and easy method to select or deselect all objects in your composition: From the Edit menu, choose Select All or Deselect All. You can alternatively use the quick keys—Ctrl+A and Shift+Ctrl+A for Windows users, or Cmd+A and Cmd+Shift+A for Mac users.

Choosing a Hidden Object

When you are working with layered objects that include a number of different objects, you may need to choose an object for editing that is not conveniently located on top of the others. The Drag-Selection tool is used to select hidden objects.

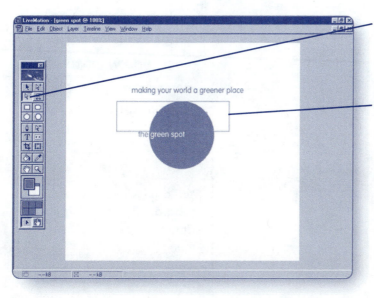

1. Click the Drag-Selection tool. The pointer changes to a crosshair.

2. Drag a marquee around the group of objects that includes the object you want to select. The hidden objects appear selected and you can now work with them as desired.

TIP

You may not want to work with every item you selected. To deselect one object in a group, press Shift (both Windows and Mac users) while you click the object.

Selecting a Subgroup

The Subgroup Selection tool is the most specialized of the selection tools. When you want to work with multiple objects but want to select each object individually, use these steps:

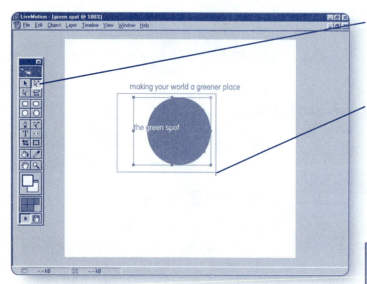

1. Click the Subgroup Selection tool. The pointer changes to a crosshair.

2. Drag the selection pointer to include the objects you want to select. One at a time, the objects are selected.

TIP

You can later reverse a subgroup by choosing Ungroup from the Object menu.

NOTE

Editing, in LiveMotion, means changing objects by resizing, rotating, aligning, and skewing them. One of the great LiveMotion editing features is that there is an Undo feature that is as far-reaching as your computer's memory can support—you can always reverse a change you made, no matter how long ago you edited the object by opening the Edit menu and choosing Undo or by pressing Ctrl+Z (Windows) or Cmd+Z (Macintosh).

Making Duplicates and Aliases

There is no reason to re-create an object when you can simply copy and modify one that you've already created. You can make a copy of LiveMotion objects two ways using these steps:

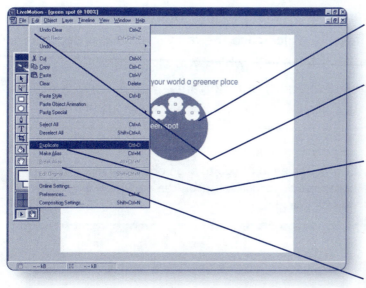

1. Select the object(s) you want to duplicate.

2. Choose Edit and then choose the command to perform the task you need:

• Duplicating the object makes an exact copy and places it on top of the original.

• Creating an alias makes a linked copy so that any changes you make to the original or an alias are reflected in both objects.

TIP

What's the difference between a duplicate and an alias? An *alias* in LiveMotion is a copy that is linked to the original object. This means that if you make a change to one object, the change affects both objects. For example, perhaps you've created a number of buttons for a Web page and now want to make a single, uniform change to all of them. Using an alias enables you to easily change them all at the same time.

Aligning Objects

Alignment, and the lack of it, are both important elements in design. In one project, having everything symmetrical communicates just the sort of straight, ordered, with-it kind of message you want. For others, you may want more of a chaotic effect, in which case the misalignment of objects (or the careful way in which you align objects so they *look* unaligned) is important.

TIP

LiveMotion enables you to align objects along a horizontal or vertical axis. You can also easily align the objects in a group.

1. Select the objects you want to align.

2. Choose Object, Align. The Align submenu opens.

• Left. Aligns the selected objects along the left edge of the selected area.

• Right. Aligns the objects along the right edge.

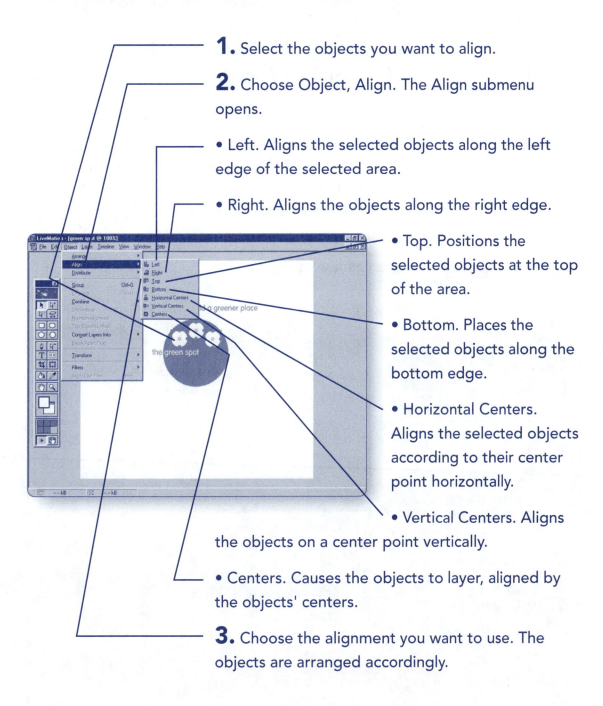

• Top. Positions the selected objects at the top of the area.

• Bottom. Places the selected objects along the bottom edge.

• Horizontal Centers. Aligns the selected objects according to their center point horizontally.

• Vertical Centers. Aligns the objects on a center point vertically.

• Centers. Causes the objects to layer, aligned by the objects' centers.

3. Choose the alignment you want to use. The objects are arranged accordingly.

Moving, Resizing, and Cropping Objects

You will often modify your LiveMotion composition by moving, resizing, and cropping objects. These tasks enable you to change images and objects you draw and import, selecting only the portions you need to use, resizing them to fit, and placing them in the right spot in your composition.

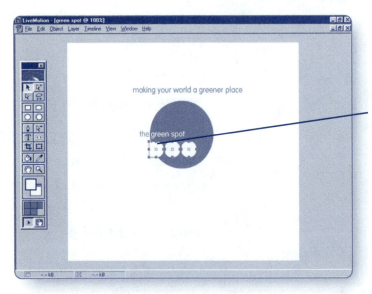

To move an object:

1. Click on the object to select it.

2. Drag the object to the new location.

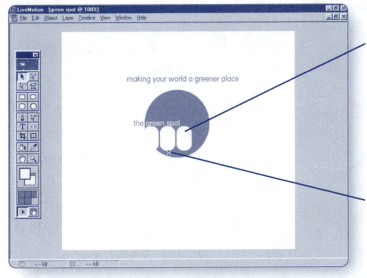

To resize an object:

1. Click on the object you want to resize. Handles appear along its outer edges and the pointer changes to a double-headed arrow.

2. Drag the handle to the desired size.

NOTE

If you want to resize the object and keep it in proportion, press and hold Shift while dragging the object handle.

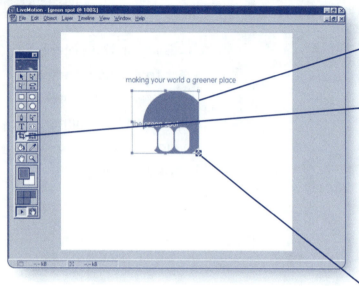

To crop an object:

1. Click on the object you want to crop.

2. Click on the Crop tool. When you position the pointer over the image, the pointer changes to a white hand with a crop symbol on the back until it is over a handle.

3. Position the pointer on one of the handles along the edge of image you want to crop.

4. Drag the object border inward.

Grouping and Ungrouping Objects

After an object appears just the way you want it, you may want to group the item so that it is part of a bigger composition that combines multiple layers, shapes, and images. This allows you to move and manipulate the group as a single object.

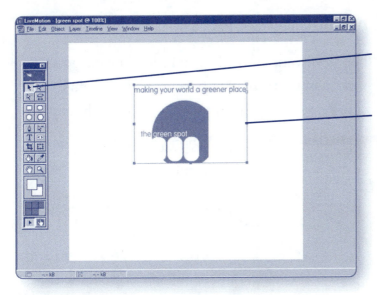

To group objects:

1. Click on the selection tool you want to use.

2. Drag a marquee around the objects you want to select. The items are all selected.

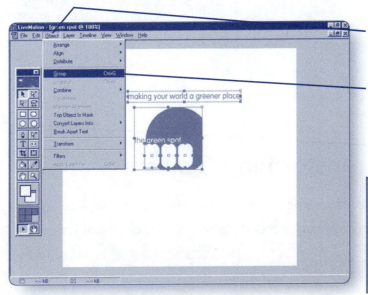

3. Click on Object. The Object menu appears.

4. Click on Group. The grouped objects are now marked as one object.

TIP

Use the Subgroup Selection tool to select individual items for editing that reside within a group.

Ungrouping Objects

When you want to work with individual objects, it can be easiest to *ungroup* the set of objects that you previously grouped together. Here's how:

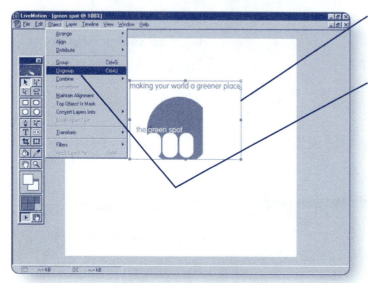

1. Click on the object you want to ungroup.

2. Click on Objects and then click on Ungroup. The objects are separated and each now appears with its own selected boundaries.

Transforming Objects

Transforming objects enables you to flip, skew, or rotate them according to their anchor points.

NOTE

The *anchor point* is the center of geometric objects. The anchor point for text objects is known as the *justification point* and is the baseline for the first line of text.

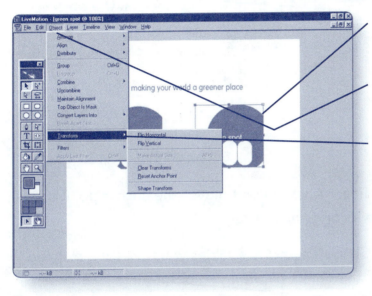

1. Select the object you want to transform.

2. Click on Objects. The Objects menu appears.

3. Click on Transform. The submenu appears.

4. Click the type of transformation you want. The objects are moved based on the command you choose.

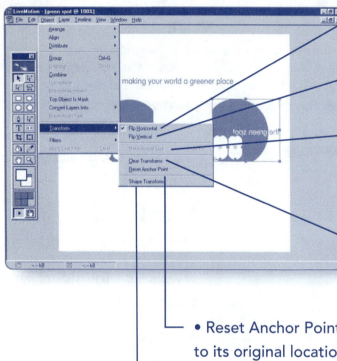

• Flip Horizontal reverses the object to the right.

• Flip Vertical reverses the object upward.

• Make Actual Size resizes the object so that it will look the same as it will on the Web.

• Clear Transforms returns the image to its original position and size.

• Reset Anchor Point moves the anchor point back to its original location.

• Shape Transform enables you to skew the shape of the object by dragging or rotating.

CAUTION

If you have selected a number of objects rather than a group and then choose Objects, Transform, it's important to remember that each object in the group will be transformed individually. For example, if a grouped object is flipped horizontally, any small ovals in the group are simply flipped horizontally in place. They are not flipped to the other side of the object in the manner of a text object.

Making Simple Modifications

Getting an image to appear just the way you want it may involve first creating the object and then playing with it or modifying it until the right shape, color, depth, and contrast are reached.

Changing Color from Outline to Fill

When you first draw a shape using LiveMotion's shape tools, the object appears in outline form. To change the outside color so that the entire object is filled, use the Properties palette.

NOTE

LiveMotion allows you to create layers upon layers of objects (up to 98 total) to get just the effect you want. This means that you may be coloring, resizing, or transforming objects on multiple layers at the same time.

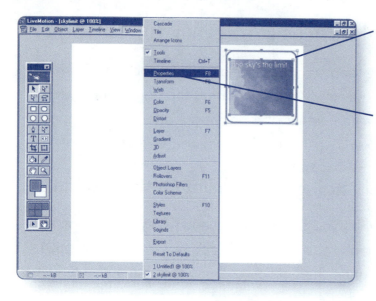

1. Click on the object you want to modify. Handles appear along its edges.

2. If the Properties palette is not visible, click on Window and then click on Properties. The Properties palette appears. The options you see in the Properties palette may vary, depending on the type of object you have selected. These are the options for the selected object in this example:

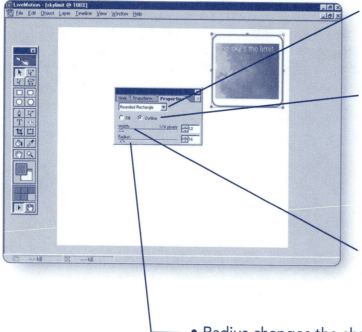

• Object selection allows you to choose the object you want to modify.

• Fill/Outline enables you to determine whether the color usage should affect only the outline of the object or the interior of the object.

• Width controls the thickness (in pixels) of the outline.

• Radius changes the shape of the object relative to the center point of the item.

TIP

When dealing with different sorts of objects, LiveMotion will show other options in the Properties palette. For now, the choices involve the color and shape of the selected object.

TIP

If you want to change the color scheme for a selected object, open the Color Scheme palette by clicking Window, Color Scheme. You can then modify the color selections as needed.

Deleting Objects

Don't like it anymore? Are you sure? Then delete it. Use these steps:

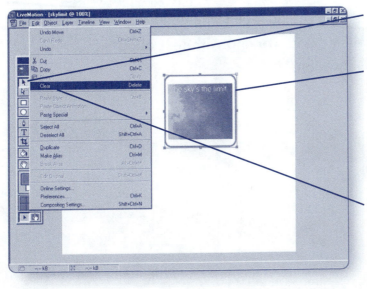

1. Click on the Selection tool.

2. Click on the object you want to delete.

3a. Press the Delete key.

OR

3b. Click on Edit, and then click on Clear. The object is deleted.

> **TIP**
>
> You can undo an accidental deletion by pressing Ctrl+Z (Windows users) or Cmd+Z (Mac users).

> **NOTE**
>
> What if you really mess things up? You can revert to the last saved version of the file. To do so, click on File, Revert. The previous version of the file becomes the current version.

A Quick Summary

This chapter has given you an overview of editing and transforming your LiveMotion objects. Specifically, you learned how select objects and then move, align, resize, duplicate, and modify them. In the next chapter, you concentrate on creating and working with text objects in LiveMotion.

7

Working with Text in LiveMotion

Take a look at the Web, and what do you see? Special text treatments—moving text, funky text, shadowed text, layered characters ghosting in the background of a contemporary design. Text in art can add strength to your message as well as visual impact to your graphical display. This chapter shows you how to create and work with text objects in LiveMotion. In this chapter, you'll learn how to

- ⬤ Create a text object.
- ⬤ Choose a font.
- ⬤ Select the text style.
- ⬤ Select text size.
- ⬤ Resize text by dragging.
- ⬤ Space text.
- ⬤ Control text alignment.

Creating a Text Object

The text you create in LiveMotion is not regular text, but rather a graphic object. The characters themselves are art and the words you create can be selected, modified, transformed, and animated like any other graphic object. The text objects are vector images, which means you can resize and skew them with no loss of clarity.

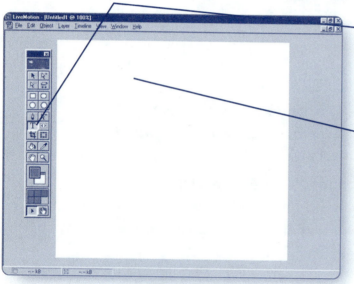

1. Click on the Text tool in the Tools palette. The pointer changes to an I-beam pointer.

2. Click on the composition area. The Type Tool dialog box appears.

The Type Tool dialog box contains all of the options you need for working with text. You'll see this dialog box when you create a new text object or when you select an existing object. Here's an overview of the options in this dialog box:

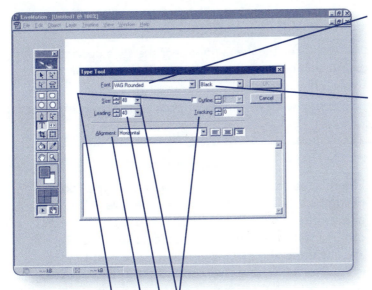

• **Font** enables you to choose the font you want to use for the text object.

• **Style** gives you a list of preset styles from which to choose. You may see Bold, Italic, Bold Italic, Regular, Rounded, or another font style choice in this list box, depending on the font you have selected.

• **Size** lets you set the size of the characters, from extremely small (6 points) to extremely large (72 points or larger, depending on the font).

• **Leading** controls the amount of space between the text lines in objects that use multiple lines of text.

• **Alignment** enables you to choose the way you want the text to align with other objects—horizontally, vertically, centered, top, or bottom. You can also choose whether you want the text to be left-justified, centered, or right-justified.

• **Outline** determines whether the characters appear as outline characters—that is, with a white internal space and a dark (or color) outline. You can further control the spacing within the outline by increasing or decreasing the value.

• **Tracking** controls the amount of space between characters in the text object.

> **NOTE**
>
> You won't see the name *Style* near the style options, but your choices appear in the top right corner of the Type Tool dialog box.

> **NOTE**
>
> Where's the cool stuff? The options in the Type Tool dialog box are all cut-and-dried text options. What about color and motion? Palettes of specialized effects can be used to control the text objects you create. You'll learn to add more splash and movement to text in Chapter 11, "Using LiveMotion Styles," and Chapter 15, "Creating Animations."

Font Selections and Strategies

The fonts you choose for your LiveMotion compositions will have a lot to do with conveying the tone of your message. Fun, lighthearted projects might have a funky, open, or humorous font. More serious projects could have a harder, more business-like look. Well designed Web pages have a carefully selected combination of typefaces—type styles that work together well to communicate the central message of the piece.

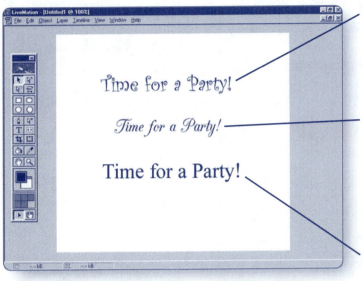

• Curlz MT is a playful font. This party could be a come-as-you-are kind of event.

• CAC Champagne is an elegant, script font. This typeface might be used on a more elegant announcement.

• Times New Roman is a traditional, serif font. This font is used often in designs for business sites and documents.

TIP

The best way to learn about the different tone that fonts convey is to keep your eyes open—you'll become aware of the typeface used on menus, on Web sites, in television advertisements, on shirts, and on movie screens. What fonts are people using to get attention? You can easily tune in by simply keeping your eyes open.

Choosing a Font

LiveMotion makes it easy for you to experiment with different fonts and try out a variety of looks.

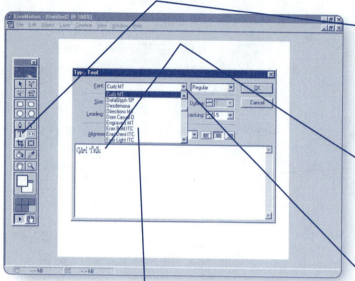

1. Click on the Type tool and then click in the composition area. The Type Tool dialog box will appear.

2. Type your text. The text will appear in the typeface displayed in the Font box.

3. Click on the Font arrow to display a list of font choices. Select the font you want to try and the result will be shown in the preview box of the Type Tool dialog box.

NOTE

The type and number of fonts you have available on your system will vary, depending on the operating system you are using and the number of additional fonts you have installed.

4. When you have the look you want, click on OK. The dialog box will close and the text object will appear on your composition.

NOTE

When you select the Type tool, LiveMotion automatically creates a copy of the last text object you created. The object appears in the Type Tool dialog box and in the composition area where you originally clicked. When you type new text in the Type Tool box, the old text will be replaced.

TIP

You can use the Timeline window to animate your text and make it look as though your characters are changing from one font to another. See Chapter 15, "Creating Animations," for more details about animating text.

Styles

The style of the text is as important as the font itself—within each typeface family, you may have a wide range of choices. The most common styles are Bold, Italic, Regular, and Bold Italic, but you may also see Thin, Light, and Black.

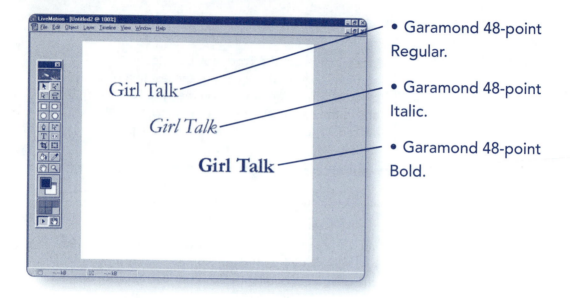

- Garamond 48-point Regular.

- Garamond 48-point Italic.

- Garamond 48-point Bold.

NOTE

Not all fonts have different styles. Some have only regular (such as Camelot), while others offer Bold, Italic, Bold Italic, and Regular.

A Quick Look at LiveMotion Styles

One of the coolest features of LiveMotion is its library of ready-made styles that you can apply to any object—text or otherwise. Take a minute now to play around with a few designer styles for your text.

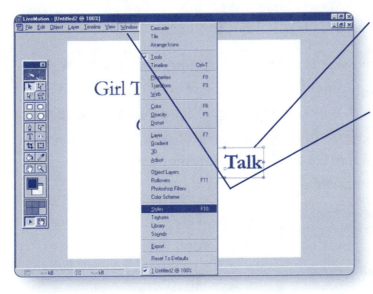

1. Click on the text object to which you want to apply the style.

2a. If necessary, click on Window and then on Styles to open the Styles palette.

OR

2b. Press F10 (Windows users) to open the Styles palette.

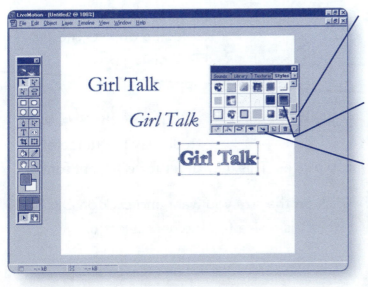

3. Scroll through the palette to find a style you want to try.

4. Click on the style icon you want.

5. Click on Apply. The style is then applied to the text object.

NOTE

You learn more about using the Styles palette in Chapter 11, "Using LiveMotion Styles."

Selecting Text Size

Text size is another fun setting to play with as you experiment with the type in your composition. Bold, oversized type scrunched into a small space, or elegant, mid-sized text, or petite, scrolled letters each make a different statement in your composition.

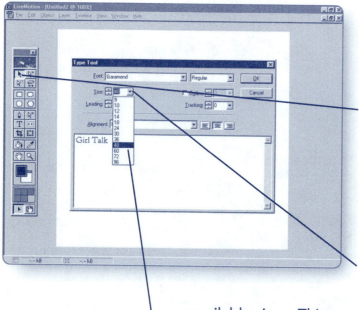

1a. Click on the Type tool.

OR

1b. Click on the Selection tool and then double-click an already-selected object. The Type Tool dialog box will appear.

2. Click on the Size arrow to display the range of available sizes. This may differ for different fonts.

3. Click on the size you want and click on OK. The text object is resized to the new selection.

TIP

If you want to create a text object that includes characters of different sizes, you need to create the characters as individual objects so that you can control their sizes individually. If you prefer, you can start with a word or phrase and then click on Object and Break Apart Text to make each character an individual object.

Resizing Text by Dragging

Because text in LiveMotion is treated as an object—and a vector object at that, which means that it is drawn based on a mathematical calculation and can be resized with no loss of clarity—you can resize text in your composition by simply clicking and dragging the handle of the object.

1. Click on the Selection tool.

2. Click on the text object you want to resize. The object is selected and handles appear along its edges.

3. Drag a handle in the direction you want to resize the object.

> **NOTE**
>
> If you want to keep the text proportional, press Shift while you drag a handle. If you will be using the same text object over and over again, ensure that your sizing is accurate by entering numeric parameters in the Type Tool dialog box.

Spacing Text

The spacing of the words and characters in your composition is another important contributor to the overall effect of the work. Leading between lines and the tracking (spacing between characters) is set in the Type Tool dialog box.

Controlling Leading

Leading determines the amount of space between the text you are creating and another line of text. You can add space to spread out text lines or decrease space to tighten things up. Again, you have a wide range of spacing choices that are related to the size of the font you have chosen.

> **NOTE**
>
> You can continue to refine your requirements in the custom AutoFilter dialog box. For example, you could search for less than $400 and more than $350 using "And" with the additional text boxes.

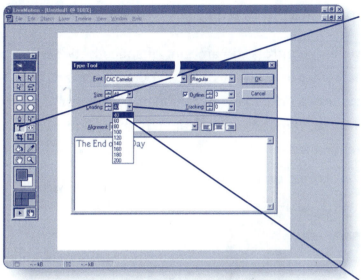

1. Click on the Type tool or double-click an existing text object to display the Type Tool dialog box.

2. Click on the Leading arrow. A range of leading choices appears. The range will vary, depending on the font and type size of the object.

3. Click on the leading value you want. Space will be added before and after the text to increase the spacing between any previous and subsequent lines of text.

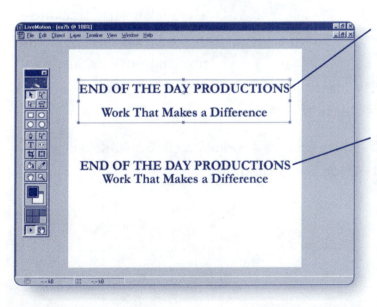

• In this first example, Garamond text is set to 30 points, Bold. The leading is set to 180.

• In this example, the Garamond 30-point Bold text is set with a leading of 100.

Choosing Tracking

Tracking controls the amount of space between characters in the text object. You can increase the amount to add space between characters or decrease it (even into negative numbers) to pull text characters closer to each other.

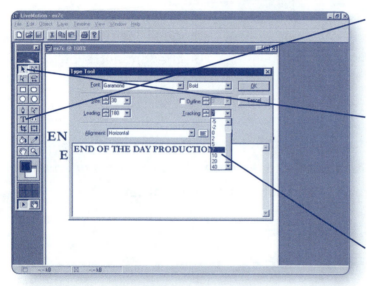

1a. Click on the Type tool.

OR

1b. Click on the Selection tool and then double-click an existing text object to display the Type Tool dialog box.

2. Click on the Tracking arrow to display the list of tracking options. You can also use the option buttons to increase or decrease the value.

3. Make your selection and click on OK to close the Type Tool dialog box.

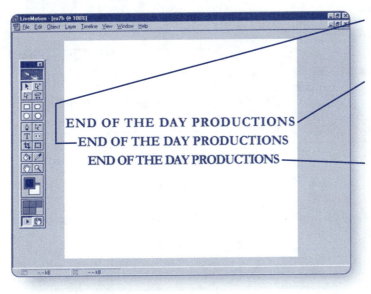

• The text object with Tracking set to 0.

• The object with Tracking set to 7. Notice the added space between characters.

• The object with Tracking set to –7. Much of the white space between characters has been removed.

Controlling Text Alignment

When you want to change the direction of text—moving it from horizontal to vertical, for instance—use LiveMotion's Alignment feature.

Alignment enables you to choose the way you want the text to be positioned with other objects—horizontally, vertically, or aligned to the center, top, or bottom edges. You can also choose whether you want the text to be left-justified, centered, or right-justified within the object.

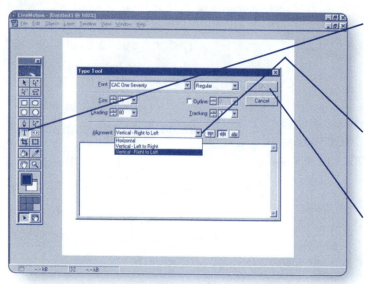

1. Click on the text object you want to change using the Text tool. The Type Tool dialog box appears.

2. Click on the Alignment arrow. The list of choices appears.

3. Make your selection and click on OK.

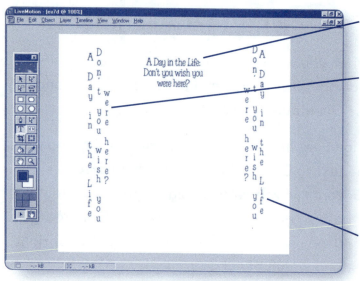

• The text object with Horizontal alignment.

• The object with Vertical—Left to Right alignment. With this type of alignment, subsequent lines of text appear to the right of the first line.

• The object with Vertical—Right to Left alignment. With this alignment, each line of text after the first one appears to the left of the earlier line.

When you think of the term *alignment*, you may think of traditional left-justified, centered, or right-justified text. LiveMotion also includes these options.

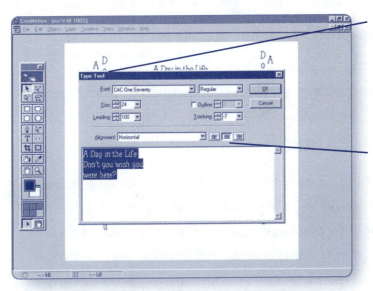

1. Click on the selection tool and then double-click the text object you want to change. The Type Tool dialog box opens.

2. Click on the alignment icon you want; then click on OK.

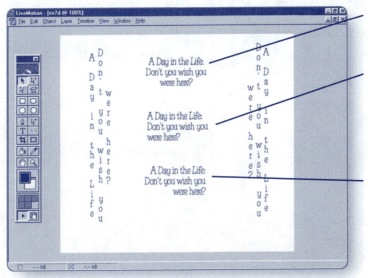

• The text is centered within the object frame.

• The text is left-justified so that the text aligns along the left edge of the object.

• The text is right-justified, meaning the text aligns along the right edge of the object.

> **TIP**
>
> You can animate individual text characters by breaking them apart and assigning movement to them using the Timeline window. Start by selecting the object and then breaking the text object into characters by clicking Object and Break Apart Text. Each letter then appears with its own set of handles, and can be selected and animated individually. To find out how to animate an object, see Chapter 15, "Creating Animations."

A Quick Summary

This chapter has explored ways you can enter and use text in your LiveMotion creations. You learned how to create text objects; set the font, style, and size you want; and control spacing and alignment. The next chapter explores the important ability to create, modify, and work with layers in your LiveMotion objects.

8

Creating and Using Layers

Compositions in LiveMotion are made up of different types of objects—images, text, shapes, and sounds. When you create an object, it occupies one layer. You have the potential to add 98 additional layers, each with its own special characteristic. This chapter shows you how to display, add, and work with object layers. Specifically, you'll learn how to

- Work with the Object Layers palette.
- Hide and redisplay layers.
- Create, copy, and arrange layers.
- Name and delete layers.
- Change layer attributes.

What Are Object Layers in LiveMotion?

Each individual object in LiveMotion can have up to 99 different layers. Those layers might include shadows, background, color, and other attributes you apply to an image to give it the depth you want. Your object may be only a single layer or it may have multiple layers, each of which adds another effect such as lighting, shadow, a glow, or a pattern.

For example, here the text overlaps the scanned image. But the image actually has multiple layers that were added through special effects in LiveMotion.

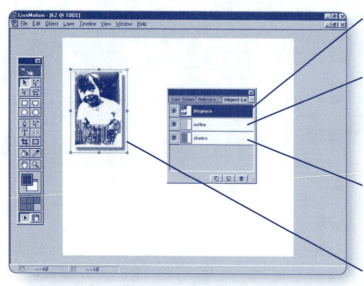

• The scanned image takes up the first layer.

• A gray border was added to the image and it was placed on the second layer.

• The dark gray shadow was added last and it occupies the third layer.

• The text is not part of this object's layers; it is a separate object.

By removing the additional layers, you can see at a glance how much the extra characteristics assigned to the object layers contributed to the object's overall appearance.

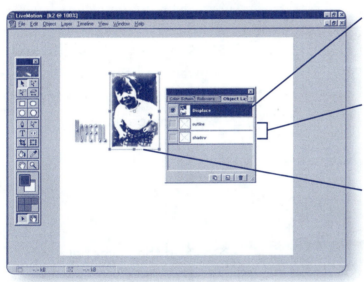

• The scanned object is the only layer visible in the selected object.

• The additional characteristics have been temporarily hidden.

• The scanned object has been moved away from the text object, which has its own layers.

Displaying Object Layers

The Object Layers palette is used to display the various layers in a selected object. To display the object layers for a specific object, use these steps:

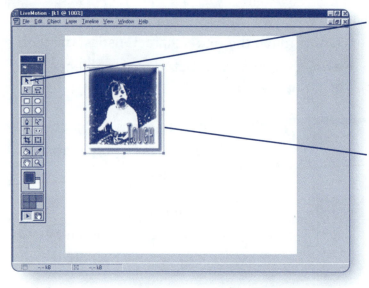

1. Click on the Selection tool. The pointer changes to an arrow when it's positioned over a selectable object.

2. Click on the object you want to use. Handles appear along the edges of the image, indicating that it is selected.

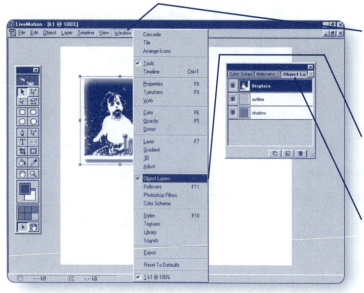

3. If the Layer palette is not visible, click on Window. The Window menu will appear.

4. Click on Object Layers. The Object Layers palette opens.

5. The individual entries in the Object Layers palette show the layers created for the selected object.

Changing Object Display

Individual layers are unique to each object and independent of each other. Therefore, when you select an object, the layers applicable to that object appear in the Object Layers palette.

As you see here, the text object, which was treated with a LiveMotion style, includes four different layers:

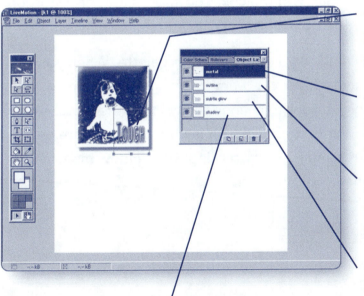

• The selected text object is actually a collection of four different layers.

• The metal layer is the most basic layer, the style applied to the text object.

• The outline layer is part of the special style applied to the text.

• The subtle glow is a color treatment, on yet another layer, that seems to shine from behind the text object.

• The shadow is the final layer, added to give a three-dimensional effect to the text.

The Difference between Object Layers and Layer Attributes

The Object Layers palette allows you to organize, move, hide, display, add, and delete the layers for individual objects. You may notice that you can't actually do much with the layers in the Object Layers palette. For example, where are the choices for changing the color, position, skew, or distortion of the object layers?

The answer lies in the Layer palette. When you have a layer you want to change (for example, you might want to change the color of the metal layer in the text object), display the Layer palette by pressing F7 or by clicking the Window menu and then clicking Layer.

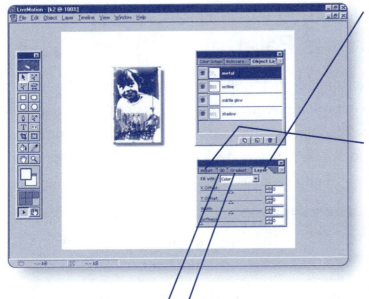

• The Layer tab enables you to choose the way the layer is positioned relative to the other layers on the object.

• The Adjust tab enables you to control brightness, contrast, saturation, and tint. You can also invert the image. (This option is not available for all types of objects, however.)

• The 3D tab gives you options for the type of 3D treatment assigned to the object and enables you to choose the positioning angle.

• The Gradient tab controls the pattern and shading of the gradient color used in the fill of the selected layer.

NOTE

For more about working with individual layer attributes, see "Changing Layer Attributes," later in this chapter.

Working with the Object Layers Palette

The on-and-off toggles in LiveMotion make it easy to experiment with different looks and layers. All the changing you do with layering in LiveMotion is also nondestructive, which means you can undo any change and recover anything you lost.

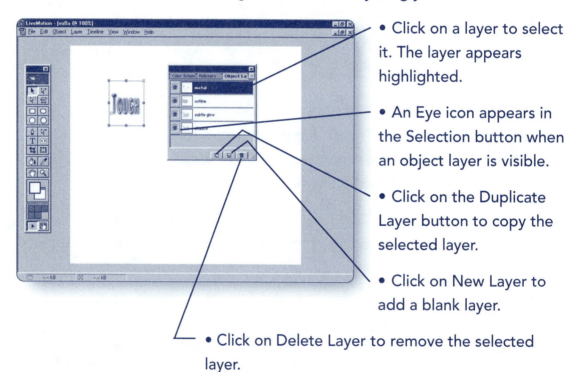

• Click on a layer to select it. The layer appears highlighted.

• An Eye icon appears in the Selection button when an object layer is visible.

• Click on the Duplicate Layer button to copy the selected layer.

• Click on New Layer to add a blank layer.

• Click on Delete Layer to remove the selected layer.

> **TIP**
>
> Don't see any object layers named in the Object Layers palette? If you have grouped your objects, no object layers will be visible to LiveMotion. Click on the Object menu and then Ungroup to display the individual objects. Then, when you display the Object Layers palette, the layers will be listed.

Hiding and Redisplaying Layers

One good way to learn about LiveMotion effects and the way in which layers alter the display of an object is to deconstruct it. For example, you might want to disassemble an object you created from LiveMotion's library or one you enhanced using a style from the Style palette. You can experiment with hiding and redisplaying layers to see how the object is affected.

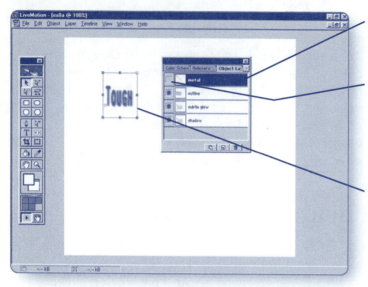

1. Click on the layer you want to hide.

2. Click on the Eye button to the left of the layer name. An "X" replaces the thumbnail image.

3. The change is made in the displayed image.

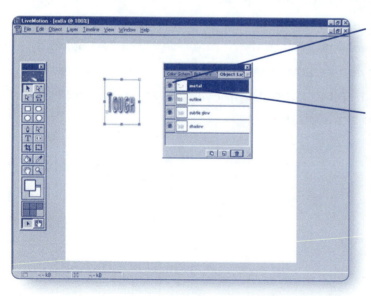

4. Click on the Selection button to redisplay the layer.

5. The Eye icon appears on the button and the thumbnail view is available again.

Creating, Copying, and Arranging Layers

For some LiveMotion objects, you may want to make several duplicates of a layer and then offset it slightly and change its color to create shadows, backdrops, highlights, or another special effect. The process for creating, copying, and arranging layers is easy—and you can always undo all the changes you make.

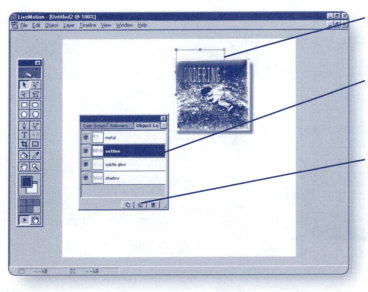

1. Click on the object to select it.

2. Click on the layer after which the new layer will be created.

3. Click on the New Layer button. A new layer is added after the previously selected layer.

Now that you have added a new layer, you can add a shape, background, or other item to the new layer to enhance the object.

> **NOTE**
>
> If you press Del when you only meant to remove a layer, the entire object containing the layer is deleted. Recover the object by clicking on Edit and then Undo.

Copying Layers

There are a number of ways to copy a layer or a layer attribute from one object to another. It would be nice to simply click and drag a layer from one object to another, but unfortunately there are a few more steps to it than that.

One method of copying is to use the Duplicate Layer button.

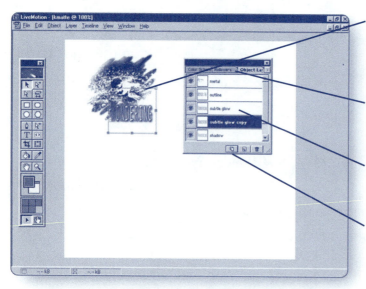

1. Click on the object that contains the layer you want to copy.

2. Open the Object Layers palette.

3. Click on the layer to be copied.

4. Click on Duplicate Layer. A copy of the selected layer is created and is listed immediately following the layer you selected in Step 1.

TIP

The most important thing to remember when copying a layer from one object to another is to be sure that you have already created a new layer in the target object. Otherwise, the copied layer will replace the existing layer, thereby giving you an unexpected result.

Copying a Layer from One Object to Another

If you want to copy a specific layer to another object, the process involves first making a copy of a specific layer and then pasting it into another object. Begin by displaying the object that contains the layer to be copied.

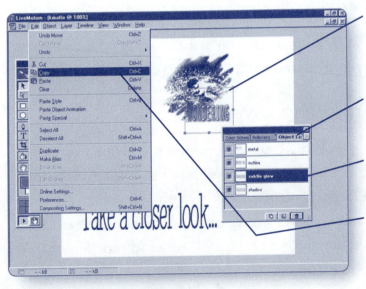

1. Click on the object that contains the layer you want to copy.

2. Open the Object Layers palette.

3. Click on the layer to be copied.

4. Click on the Edit menu and then click Copy. The object is placed in the clipboard.

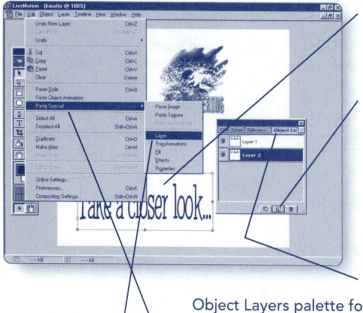

5. Click on the object to which you want to add the layer.

6. Click on the New Layer button to add a new layer in the receiving object; otherwise, the incoming layer will replace the currently selected layer in the receiving object.

7. If necessary, open the Object Layers palette for the receiving object.

8. Click on the Edit menu and then click on Paste Special. A submenu will appear.

9. Click on Layer. The attribute from the copied layer is pasted to the selected object.

Arranging Layers

The way in which you arrange the layers in your object can make a big difference in the overall look of the composition. For example, if you put a shadow in the wrong place, or layer a darker accent over a lighter one, you will need to reorder what you've done.

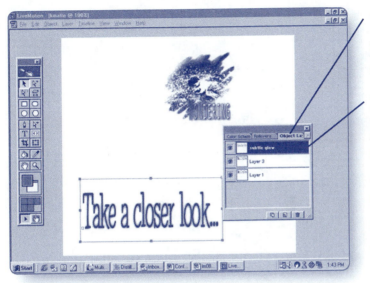

1. Click on the layer you want to move in the Object Layers palette.

2. Drag the layer to a new location and release the mouse button. The layers are reordered with the layer moved to the new spot. The selected object will display the changes.

NOTE

Which order is which? The first layer listed in the Object Layers palette is the topmost layer with each subsequent layer listed sequentially.

Naming and Deleting Layers

LiveMotion plugs in its own names when you add a new layer to your object, naming them Layer 1, Layer 2, and so on. You can easily rename the layers you create.

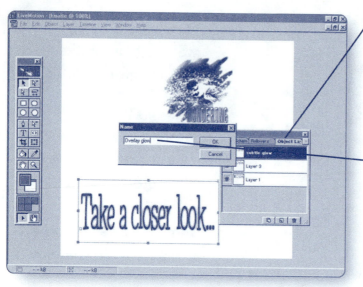

1. On the Object Layers palette, double-click on the layer you want to rename. The Name dialog box will appear.

2. Type a new name for the layer and click on OK. The layer name is changed on the Object Layers palette.

A final stopping point for layer handling: deletion. When you want to delete a layer you've created, it's a two-step process:

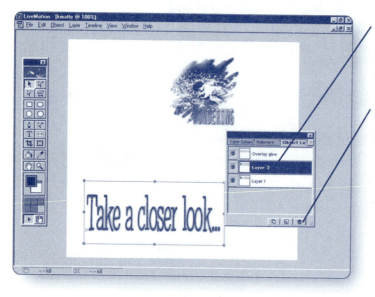

1. Click on the layer you want to delete in the Object Layers palette.

2. Click on the Delete Layer button.

> **NOTE**
>
> As always, you can recover the deleted layer by clicking on Undo Delete Layer in the Edit menu.

Changing Layer Attributes

Throughout this chapter, you've learned about working with individual layers—moving them, copying them, creating them, and deleting them. This type of manipulation has nothing to do with changing the actual *attributes* of the layers themselves, however. You'll use the Layer palette to do this.

The Layer palette gives you a number of methods to further fine-tune your object layers. Here is a look at the first tab in the Layer Attributes palette, which deals specifically with layer content and placement.

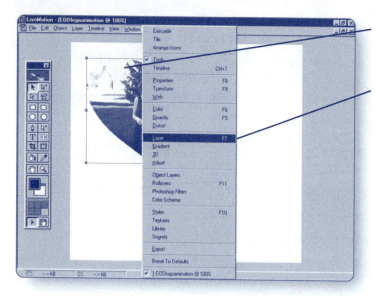

1. Click on the object you want to modify.

2. If the Layer palette is not visible, click on the Edit menu and then click on Layer. This will open the Layer palette.

NOTE

If you are working with an object that has more than one layer, you'll need to open the Object Layers palette to select the layer you want to work with.

- Click on the Fill with arrow to select the method in which the layer is filled (Color, Image, Background, or Texture).

- Drag the X Offset marker to move the layer horizontally.

- Drag the Y Offset marker to move the layer vertically.

- Drag the Width marker to make the layer wider or narrower.

- Drag the Softness marker to the right to increase the softness of the layer edges.

NOTE

You can continue to refine your requirements in the custom AutoFilter dialog box. For example, you could search for less than $400 and more than $350 using "And" with the additional text boxes.

A Quick Summary

This chapter introduced you to using, arranging, and working with layers in your LiveMotion objects. Specifically, you learned how to use the Object Layers palette to hide, display, create, copy, and arrange layers. You also discovered how to name, delete, and change layer attributes. The next chapter tackles the task of choosing and assigning colors for your LiveMotion objects.

9

Selecting Colors for Compositions

Have you ever complimented a friend by saying, "That sweater is a cool shade of green..." only to have him look at you oddly and say, "Thanks, but it's blue!"

Color is like that; it often is interpreted in the eye of the beholder. Our eyes register each color differently. Our computer monitors, printers, and Web browsers do, too.

This chapter introduces you to the use of color in LiveMotion. From the basics of how to use the tools and select the palettes, you'll learn which colors are "Web safe" and how to create your own color scheme for the display and output you choose. Specifically, in this chapter, you'll learn how to

- Apply color to your compositions.
- Work with the Color palette.
- Use Web-safe colors.
- Create and control gradients.
- Choose object opacity.
- Create a color scheme.

Applying Color

The first color change most people make in LiveMotion is the foreground or background color of the entire composition. Start by checking out the colors that are available by default:

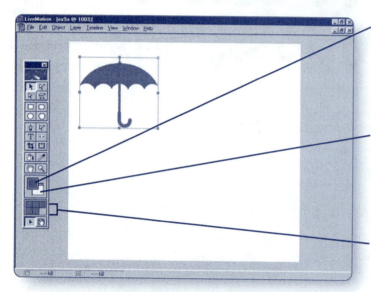

• The Foreground color (black by default) applies to the selected objects in the composition area.

• The Background color (white by default) applies to the background of the composition.

• The color palette offers five current color choices.

NOTE

The colors in the current palette remain until you change the color selections or choose a different color scheme.

Coloring the Big Picture: Background and Foreground

Changing the foreground and background colors is a simple matter of pointing and clicking.

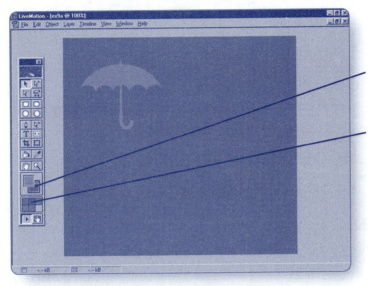

To change the background color:

1. Click on the background icon.

2. Click on the color in the palette you want to apply. The color then appears as the background of the composition.

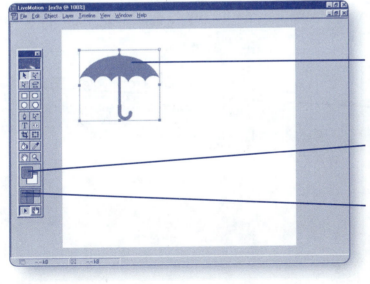

To change the foreground color:

1. Select the foreground object you want to change.

2. Click on the foreground icon.

3. Click on the color in the palette you want to apply. The color is now applied to the objects you selected in the foreground.

> ### TIP
> If you want to change the foreground colors for all objects in a composition, click on the Edit menu and then click on Select All. Then click on the foreground icon.

Choosing Colors with the Color Palette

The Color palette gives you a variety of choices for the way in which you choose the colors for your compositions. If the Color palette is not currently displayed on your screen, open it by following these steps:

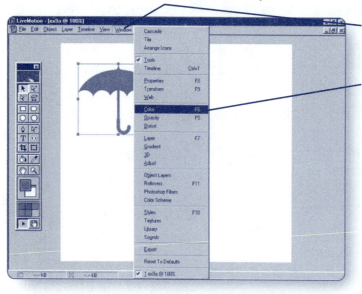

1. Click on the Window menu.

2. Click on Color. The Color palette appears.

Checking Out the Color Palette

The Color palette displays the currently selected foreground and background colors as well as the color ranges that are related to the selected color model.

NOTE

A color model is a method of creating color. LiveMotion supports six different color models, including RGB, CMYK, HSB, and CIE L. For more about choosing a different color model, see the next section, "Working with Color Models in LiveMotion."

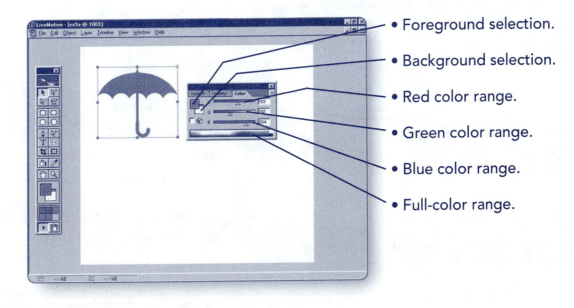

• Foreground selection.

• Background selection.

• Red color range.

• Green color range.

• Blue color range.

• Full-color range.

NOTE

To recolor a specific layer in a multilayer object, open the Window menu, choose Layers, and select the layer you want to recolor before selecting a color in the Color palette.

TIP

To display the Color palette quickly, press F6 on either Mac or Windows systems.

Changing a Color in the Color Palette

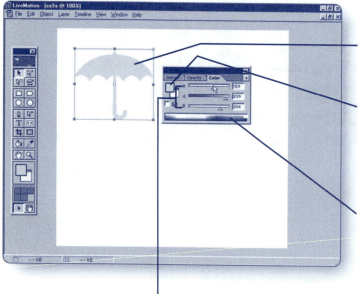

To change a color:

1. Click on the object you want to change.

2. Click either the foreground or background icon for the item you want to change.

3. Drag the pointer in the full-color range, and then click on the color you want.

4. Fine-tune the color by dragging the sliders in the Red, Green, and Blue ranges.

> **NOTE**
>
> The display in this Color palette is based upon the RGB color model. To see the options available for other available color models, refer to the next section, "Working with Color Models in LiveMotion."

> **TIP**
>
> If you know the RGB values (the numeric values for the amount of Red, Green, and Blue used to create your color) for the color you want to apply, you can type their values in the text boxes that appear to the right of the color ranges.

Working with Color Models in LiveMotion

If you are familiar with other Adobe products, such as Photoshop and Illustrator, you already know the high attention those programs give to color treatment. From the overall color tone of your page to the carefully selected combinations you use in your compositions, the colors you select will have a major impact on how well you communicate the message you're trying to convey.

LiveMotion gives you the option of working with several different color models. Specifically, you can select the following:

• **Saturation View** rates the strength of the color, measured from 0% (no color) to 100% (full color).

• **Value View** tracks the darkness (0%) to lightness (100%) of a color.

• **Hue View** shows color as it is reflected on the color wheel.

• **HSB View** mixes the color related to the hue, saturation, and brightness (hence the HSB abbreviation) of the selection.

• **RGB View** rates the intensity of red, green, and blue on a scale of 0 to 255 for each color.

• **CIE L View** shows the range of available colors in a given range.

Thinking Web-Safe

What is Web-safe? Because there are so many different types of computers used to access the Web—from ancient ones to those with cutting-edge technology—most Web designers try to create effects that will look good on the greatest number of systems. This means that even though systems are capable of displaying literally millions of colors beautifully, there is a select group of colors, termed *Web-safe colors*, that is thought to be consistently displayed on the greatest number of systems. The Web-safe palette is supported by LiveMotion, thus limiting your millions-of-colors option to 216 best bets. You'll learn how to make sure your colors are Web-safe in this chapter.

To turn on Web-safe colors:

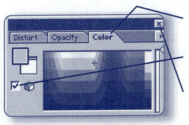

1. Display the Color palette.

2. Check the Web-safe checkbox.

3. Click the palette close box. The setting will remain in effect until you change it.

NOTE

When does LiveMotion's Web safety kick in? If you have selected the Web-safe colors checkbox in the Color palette, when you export a file LiveMotion ensures that your colors are saved in a Web-safe format (using the 215 colors that display vibrantly on the Web).

Applying Color with Your Color Tools

Two tools in the LiveMotion palette make it easy for you to "pick up" color from one object and "pour" it into another. These two tools are the Eyedropper and the Paint Bucket.

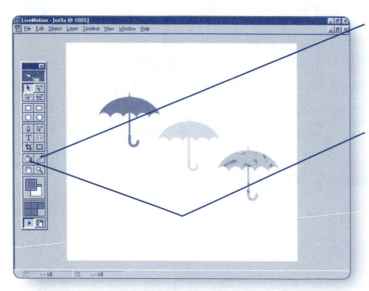

• Use the Eyedropper tool to pick up the color and/or styles you want to use in other object layers.

• Use the Paint Bucket tool to pour the effect into the selected layer.

NOTE

For either Mac or Windows users, to select the Eyedropper tool using the keyboard, press I. To choose the Paint Bucket tool, press K.

Copying Color with the Eyedropper Tool

To copy a color from one object to another:

1. Click on the layer or object you want to change.

2. Click on the Eyedropper tool. The pointer changes to an Eyedropper icon.

3. Click on the object or layer with the color you want to copy. The new color fills the selected object.

TIP

To copy a style from one object to another, press the Shift key while you click the Eyedropper tool on the style you want to copy. The selected object will be given the new style. A style is a preset design you can apply to your objects. For more about working with LiveMotion styles, see Chapter 11, "Using LiveMotion Styles."

Copying Color to Multiple Objects with the Paint Bucket

Once you take a sample of a color or style using the Eyedropper tool, you can pour it into multiple layers and objects with the Paint Bucket tool.

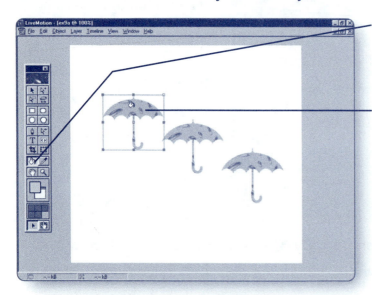

1. Click on the Paint Bucket tool. The pointer changes to a Paint Bucket.

2. Position the bucket so that it "pours into" the object you want to change and then click. Each time you click the mouse button, the color or style fills the area.

Creating and Controlling Gradients

Setting a gradient for your object layer allows you to blend two colors to get a specific effect. You might fade an image from bright to faint, light to dark, or mix in a radial effect to create a background swirl.

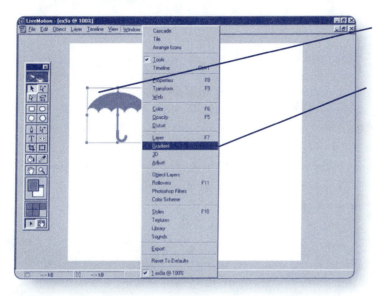

1. Select the object layer you want to change.

2. Open the Window menu and choose Gradient. The Gradient palette appears.

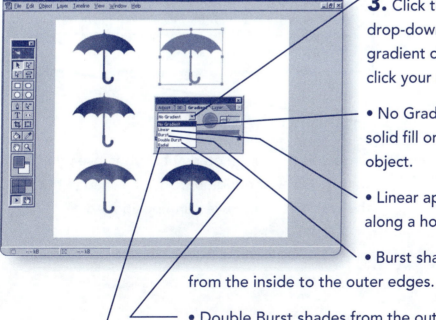

3. Click the Gradient drop-down arrow. A list of gradient choices opens; click your choice.

• No Gradient leaves a solid fill on the selected object.

• Linear applies a gradient along a horizontal line.

• Burst shades the layer from the inside to the outer edges.

• Double Burst shades from the outer edges to the center.

• Radial shades from the middle to the outer edge in a circular shape.

TIP

To make sure that the gradient you set rotates with an object, open the Object menu and choose Transform and then Shape Transform. You also need to click the Relative checkbox in the Gradient list box to ensure that the gradient is displayed relative to the position of the object.

NOTE

Even though the Web-safe color feature in the Color palette is on, using gradients may create colors that don't display properly on the Web. This is because a gradient relies on subtle and progressive color changes, and the Web-safe palette simply does not have enough colors to display all the subtle changes. Be sure to check the effects of your gradients in several browsers before letting them fly.

Changing the Gradient

Once you create the gradient in your layer, you may want to do a bit of editing. You can change the way the gradient is displayed and positioned.

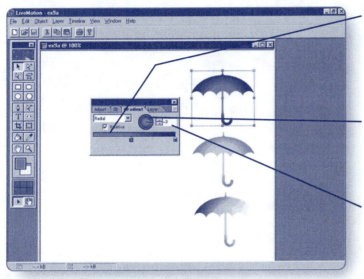

• Drag the color start and stop markers inward to change the range of color displayed in the gradient.

• Rotate the color wheel to change the way the gradient is positioned.

• Click and enter a new value to modify the percentage of color included in the gradient.

Choosing Object Opacity

Object opacity is all about transparency...how dense is the color? Will other objects show through? Object opacity can help you bring images to the forefront, making them visible and then invisible again. It can also provide subtle images behind forefront items that catch the viewer's focus most readily. To change an object's opacity, follow these steps:

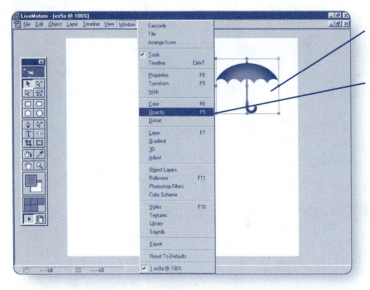

1. Click on the object you want to change.

2. Open the Window menu and choose Opacity. The Opacity palette will open.

NOTE

Before you begin, if necessary, select the layer by opening the Object Layers palette and then click on the layer you want to use.

TIP

To display the Opacity palette quickly, press F5 (both Mac and Windows users).

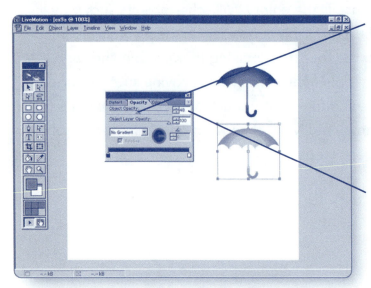

3a. Drag the Object Opacity slider to the left to decrease the density of the object. The object reflects the change.

OR

3b. Click in the text box and type a numeric for the opacity. The number you enter is a percentage, with 100 percent being opaque and 0 being transparent.

NOTE

If you were working with a single layer in an object, you would use the Object Layer Opacity slider to change the density of the selected layer.

Adding a Gradient to Opacity Changes

The Gradient option can also be used to mix and match the opacity of an object, which will cause the object to fade in and out.

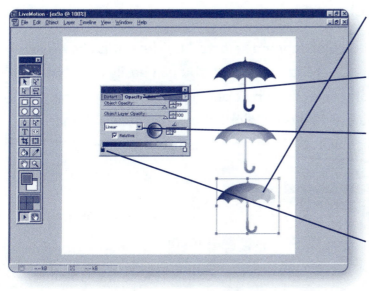

1. Select the object on which you want to work.

2. Open the Opacity palette by pressing F5.

3. Click on the Gradient drop-down arrow to reveal the Gradient choices, and then make your selection.

4. Drag the start and stop markers to set the amount of opacity you want to display.

Creating a Color Scheme

Don't have a knack for color? One designer I know says that we all have an instinctive eye for good

TIP

If you feel out of your element choosing colors that work well together, check out your resources. On the Web, there are a number of Web-color mavens with advice to help you. Additionally, you can purchase any number of books, color-modeling tools, and utilities to help you make the choices you need. The Pantone Color Matching system is one very helpful and popular guide to making sure you're choosing colors that really match.

design. The most important characteristic in good color selections is a visual awareness—a sense for seeing the fine subtleties of color, recognizing what works and what doesn't.

Learning the LiveMotion Color Scheme

The color scheme selected by default is shown in the LiveMotion toolbar. You can easily modify those color selections by opening the Color Scheme palette. If your Color Scheme palette is not visible, display it by following these steps:

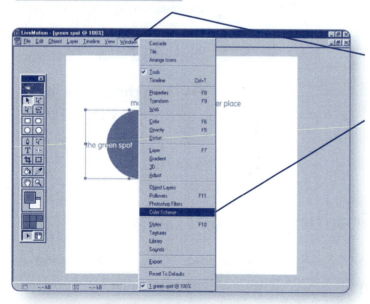

1. Open the Window menu.

2. Choose the Color Scheme palette. The palette opens.

• The color wheel shows the various colors and their relationships to each other, with the base color identified separately.

• The display area shows the palette combinations.

• Click to increase or decrease the number of colors included in the palette (the allowable range is from 2 to 6 colors).

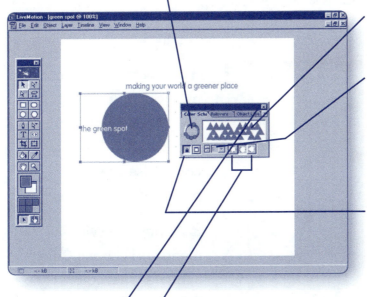

• Click on the Lock Color Scheme button to *unlock* the Color Scheme so you can make modifications.

• Choose the relationship of the colors in the palette you want to use.

TIP

You can change the way the palette colors are displayed in the Color Scheme dialog box by clicking the arrow located in the upper-right corner of the palette. A submenu appears giving you the choices of Triangles or Honeycomb. To change the display of the color choices, select Honeycomb.

Create Your Own Color Scheme

When you want to set up your own color scheme from scratch, start by choosing the base color in the Color Scheme palette.

NOTE

If you have a specific value you want to enter for the base color—perhaps an RGB or HSB color—enter those values in the Color palette.

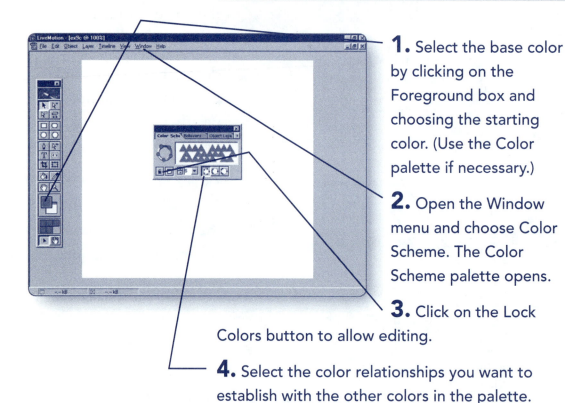

1. Select the base color by clicking on the Foreground box and choosing the starting color. (Use the Color palette if necessary.)

2. Open the Window menu and choose Color Scheme. The Color Scheme palette opens.

3. Click on the Lock Colors button to allow editing.

4. Select the color relationships you want to establish with the other colors in the palette.

TIP

Both Mac and Windows users can close all palettes quickly by pressing Tab.

A Quick Summary

In this chapter, you've learned how LiveMotion works with colors. Specifically, you've learned how to apply color to the foreground and background of your compositions. You've also found out about using the Color palette and setting object opacity and gradients. The next chapter shows you how to enhance your composition by using items from the LiveMotion Library.

10

Visiting the LiveMotion Library

Not every composition will demand that you create everything from scratch, thank goodness. Sometimes you'll use recognizable shapes, arrows, swirls, and squiggles. Other times you'll create objects that you'd like to save for use again in your work. The LiveMotion Library makes it easy for you to do both these things. In this chapter, you'll learn about the LiveMotion Library and find out how to do these tasks:

- Display and use the Library.
- Add Library objects to your composition.
- Change the Library objects you use.
- Create your own Library objects.
- Delete Library objects.

Exploring the Library

The LiveMotion Library is equipped with a number of objects and treatments you can use in your own compositions. You can also use the Library to store items you create that you plan to reuse—objects such as animations, logos, and those that contain special styles. The Library is used to store objects that you will use over and over again.

To display the LiveMotion Library, use these steps:

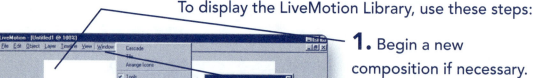

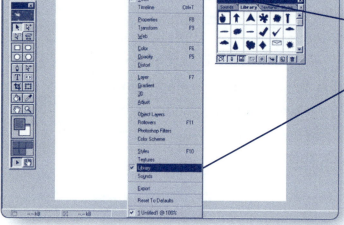

1. Begin a new composition if necessary.

2. Click on the Window menu.

3. Click on Library. The LiveMotion Library palette opens.

TIP

You aren't limited to saving simple symbols and objects to your LiveMotion Library. You can save the animation you've created, a rollover effect, or even a custom sound. Anything you think you will use in future compositions can be saved easily in the LiveMotion Library.

The LiveMotion Library includes a number of
features that help you select and work with Library
objects:

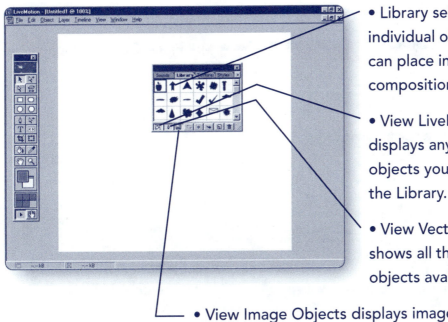

• Library selections are
individual objects that you
can place in your
compositions.

• View LiveMotion Objects
displays any LiveMotion
objects you have added to
the Library.

• View Vector Objects
shows all the vector
objects available.

• View Image Objects displays images saved as
objects in the Library.

• Replace Object enables you to replace one object with another object.

• Make Active Matte turns a selected object into a mask for a selected photo or image.

• Place Object enables you to insert the object you select into the composition.

• New Object opens a dialog box so that you can add an object to the Library.

• Delete Object removes the selected Library object.

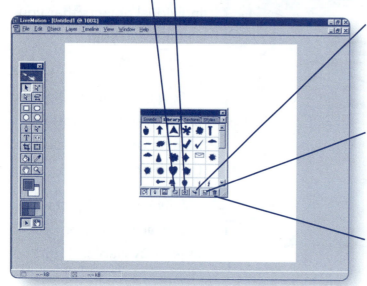

Resizing the Library

You can change the size of the Library to display all the selections at once. Simply position the double-headed pointer on the bottom border of the Library and drag it down to reveal all objects.

Changing the Library Selection

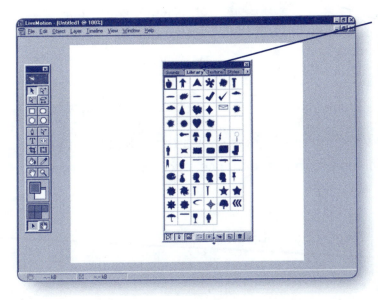

You can also use the Library display buttons to limit or increase the number of objects displayed in the Library. When you first display the Library, you'll see the collection of a number of different images. But by using the different display buttons, you can see which objects belong to which groups:

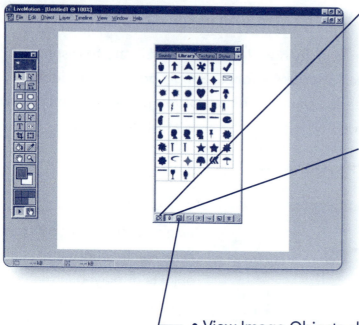

- View LiveMotion Objects displays only one image by default, but this is where any objects you add to the Library will appear.

- View Vector Objects displays the largest group of objects, which are vector-based, drawing-type graphics comprised of shapes and curves that are based on calculations

- View Image Objects shows the images that you will use to matte, enhance, and modify objects.

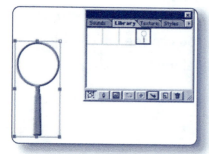

LiveMotion Objects

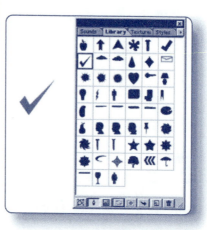

Vector Objects

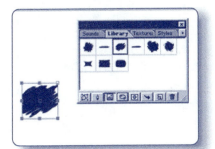

Image Objects

Adding Library Objects to a Composition

As you look at the Library offerings, you'll find some shapes that you can use as is while other shapes will require modification. The first step, no matter what you plan to do with the object, is to place it in your composition.

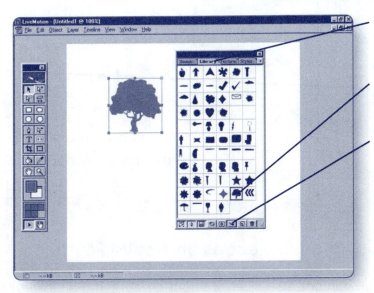

1. Open the Library palette.

2. Click on the Library object you want to use.

3. Click on the Place button. The object will be placed in the composition window.

> **TIP**
> You can also place the object in your composition quickly by simply dragging it from the Library palette and dropping it in the work area.

Replacing an Object

Once you put an object in your composition, you may decide it isn't exactly what you wanted and decide to replace it with another one.

1. Select the object you want to replace.

2. Open the Library palette.

3. Click on the new object you want to use.

4. Click on the Replace Object button.

The object is then replaced with the new selection.

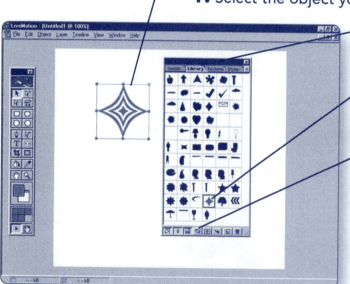

Using an Object as an Active Matte

You can create a special effect by applying a Library object as an active matte along with other objects in LiveMotion. For example, you might

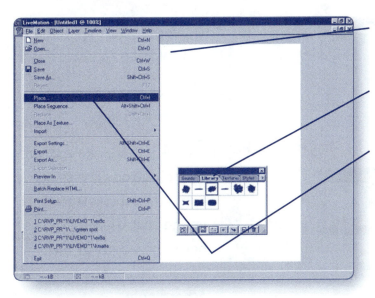

1. Begin a new composition.

2. Display the Library palette.

3. Open the File menu and choose Place.

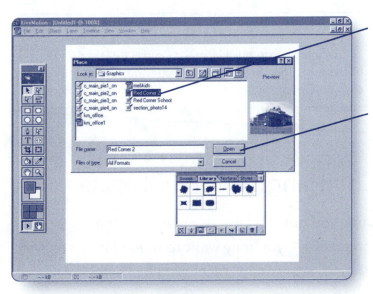

4. Select the image you want to use with the matte.

5. Click on Open to add the image to the composition.

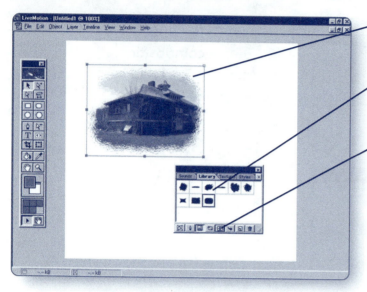

6. Verify that the image is still selected.

7. Click the matte style you want to apply.

8. Click the Make Active Matte button. The shape is applied to the selected image and, as you can see here, the edges of the image are changed accordingly.

TIP

To place an image quickly, press Cmd+I (Mac) or Ctrl+I (Windows). Then select the file you want to use and click on Open.

Changing Library Objects

Once you get the Library object into the composition, you may want to modify it by resizing, rotating, skewing, or recoloring it.

Resizing Objects

Resizing an object is simple using the traditional click-and-drag technique. Alternatively, you can

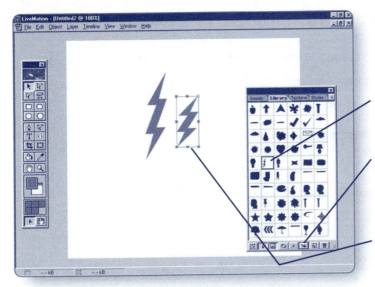

open the Transform palette and enter size-specific values.

1. Select the Library object you want to use.

2. Click on the Place button to add it to the composition.

3. Drag one of the handles of the selected object in the direction you want the object to be resized.

To resize the object by modifying the width and height values:

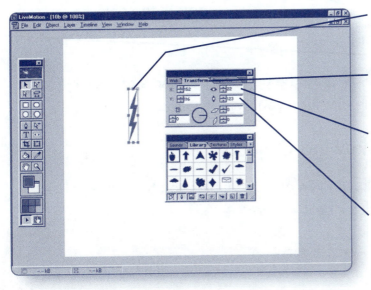

1. Select the object you want to resize.

2. Press F9 to open the Transform palette.

3. Click the Width arrows to increase or decrease the width of the object.

4. Click the Height arrows to increase or decrease the height of the object.

Rotating Objects

Rotating an object lets you turn or *spin* an object around an axis so that it best fits the image you're creating.

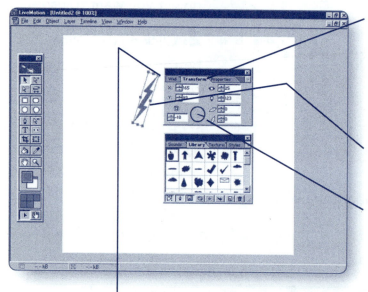

1. Open the Transform palette, if necessary, by pressing F9 or by choosing Transform from the Window menu.

2. Select the object you want to rotate.

3a. Drag the line in the object wheel in the direction you want to rotate the object.

OR

3b. Drag the upper-right handle of the object in the direction you want it to rotate.

Skewing Objects

Skewing an object enables you to slant an object for its best effect.

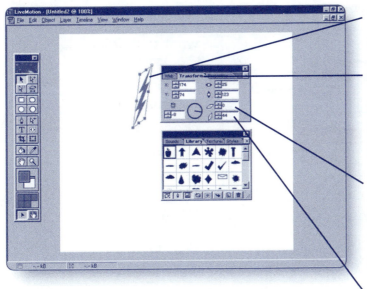

1. Select the object you want to skew.

2. Open the Transform palette by pressing F9 or by choosing Transform from the Window menu.

3. Click on the horizontal skew up or down arrows to modify the horizontal skew.

4. Click on the vertical skew up or down arrows to modify the vertical skew.

Changing Object Color

Some objects in the LiveMotion Library are assigned colors while others are black. You can assign the color, gradient, and opacity values to a Library object just as you would any LiveMotion object in your composition.

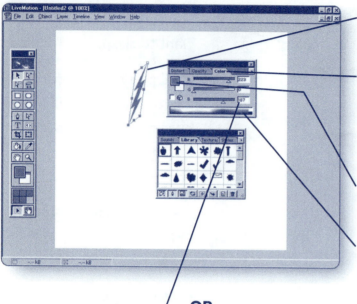

1. Select the object you want to modify.

2. Open the Color palette by pressing F6 or by choosing Color from the Window menu..

3. Click on the foreground icon.

4a. Click on the color you want to use.

OR

4b. Enter the color values that comprise the color you want

Creating Your Own Library Objects

After modifying or creating an object, you can add it to the LiveMotion Library, thus saving your hard work so that you can use it for other compositions.

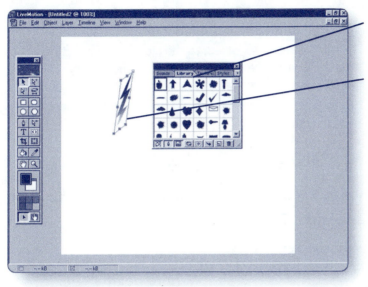

1. Open the LiveMotion Library palette.

2. Select the object you want to add to the Library.

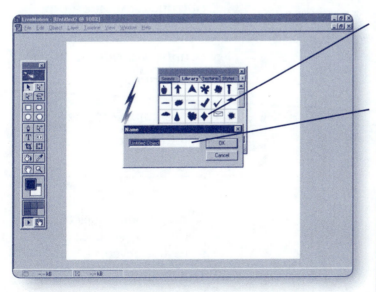

3. Drag the object to the Library. The Name dialog box will open.

4. Click in the Name box and type a name for the Library object.

NOTE

Be sure that you have selected Display LiveMotion Objects in the Library palette so that the Library objects you have added are visible.

NOTE

You can also add an object to the Library by importing a file. Click on the New Object button in the Library palette and choose the file in the Add Shape dialog box.

Deleting Library Objects

LiveMotion objects you no longer want or need can be deleted. To delete an object:

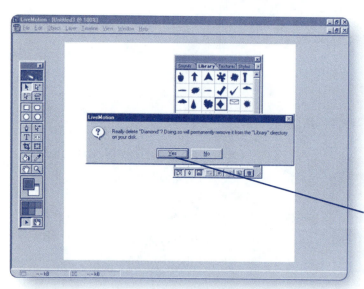

1. Select the object you want to delete.

2. Click on the Remove button. A message box appears asking you to confirm your deletion instruction.

3. To complete the deletion, click on Yes.

NOTE

You cannot "undelete" a Library object once you have removed it.

A Quick Review

This chapter has introduced you to a simple, effective LiveMotion tool: the Library. With a collection of objects that enable to you design your compositions faster, the Library adds to the flexibility of the designs you create. Specifically in this chapter, you learned how to use the Library to add, modify, and delete the LiveMotion shapes and objects ready for your use. You also found out how to add your own objects to the Library. The next chapter focuses on working with LiveMotion styles to add power and presence to your compositions.

11

Using LiveMotion Styles

As you have doubtlessly discovered, LiveMotion includes many professional elements that help you make your work look good, fast. The Styles palette is one of those features that helps you create quality objects quickly. In this chapter, you'll learn how to

- Work with the Styles palette.
- View existing styles.
- Apply styles.
- Choose a style.
- Modify styles.
- Create new styles.
- Remove styles from the palette.

Working with the Styles Palette

Styles, in LiveMotion, allow you to apply specially designed effects and formats to objects in your composition. The styles available in LiveMotion can give objects a polished, professional look, and instead of experimenting and playing with a variety of palettes to get the feel you want, you can save design time by using LiveMotion's styles and modifying them to suit your needs. You can use styles to

• Apply a color fill and gradient to a layer.

• Apply a format, style, or special effect to a text object.

• Add a particular type of drop shadow to an object.

• Apply a rollover to an object easily by using a style that has a built-in rollover effect.

• Animate the object with a predesigned animation or one that you create yourself.

Working with styles in LiveMotion involves the use of the Styles palette. The Styles palette stores the styles that are included with LiveMotion. You'll find styles that are strictly object-enhancing styles, but there are also animation, rollover, and Photoshop filter styles from which you can choose.

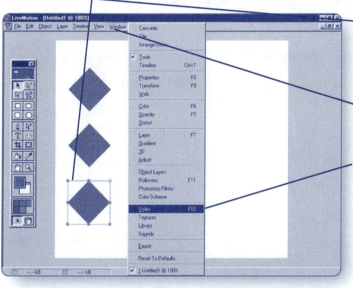

1. Select the object to which you want to apply the style.

2. Click on Window. The Window menu appears.

3. Click on Styles, if the Styles palette is not visible. The Styles palette opens.

TIP

When the Styles palette first opens, not all of the styles are visible. Resize the palette by dragging its bottom border so that you can view all of the styles at once.

Viewing Existing Styles

When you first display the Styles palette, a collection of icons, or thumbnails, appears. Some objects in the Styles palette look similar to one another; others have various colors, backgrounds, and drop shadows. Here are the various elements in the Styles palette:

• **Styles** tab, used to display available styles.

• **Styles view selector**, which enables you to choose the way the styles are displayed.

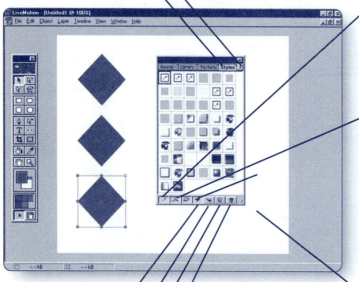

• **View Styles with Animation** acts as a toggle, displaying and then hiding the animation styles.

• **View Styles with Rollovers** is also a toggle, displaying and hiding styles that include rollover elements.

• **View Styles with Object Layers** displays and hides styles that have multiple object layers.

• **View Styles with Photoshop Filters** displays and hides the styles built from Photoshop filters.

• **Apply Style** enables you to apply the selected style to the current object.

• **New Style** displays the Name dialog box so that you can name a new style.

• **Delete Style** allows you to delete the selected style.

Choosing a View

By selecting the Styles view selector, you can choose the way in which you view the available styles. For some styles, seeing the name and preview of the style is helpful; for others, viewing the thumbnail displays it best.

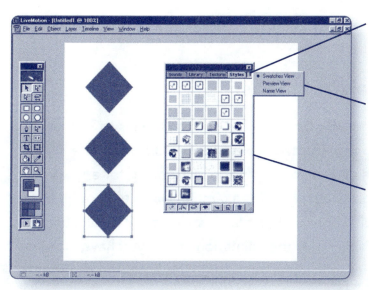

1. Click the arrow to the right of the Styles tab to display the style submenu.

2. Click the view you want to use in the Styles palette.

3. The Swatches view, which is the default, displays the styles as rows of images, or thumbnails.

• Preview view lists the various styles by name. Click on a style name to see the style previewed in the left panel.

• Name view displays the styles by name and includes the style images along the left side of the list.

Selecting Styles

The view buttons give you the means to further control the types of styles you display in the Styles palette. If you know you are looking for an animation style, for example, why sift through all the rollover and object layer styles, too? By electing to display only the animation styles, you have a clearer shot at the one you want. Here's how to change the displayed styles in the Style palette:

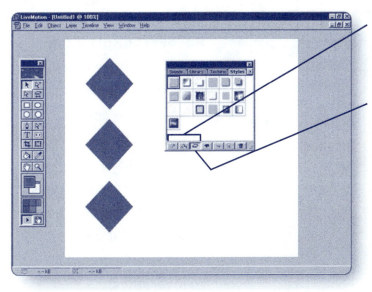

1. Review the view buttons in the bottom left of the Styles palette.

2. Click the button for the styles group you want to view.

The available styles are divided into four different groups:

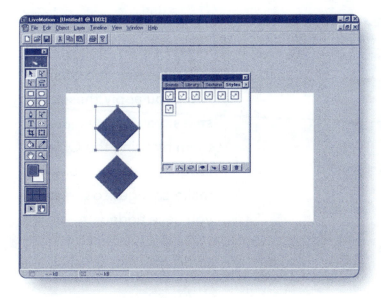

• **View Styles with Animation** shows you the styles that have animations automatically applied. You can use, modify, and save these animations to suit your own needs, of course.

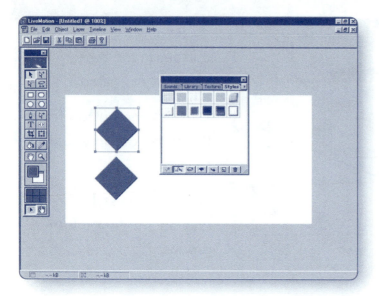

• **View Styles with Rollovers** displays the styles that have rollovers attached to them. Rollovers are special effects that play when the object is passed over by the mouse pointer. You can use animation, high color, or another type of treatment to create a rollover effect.

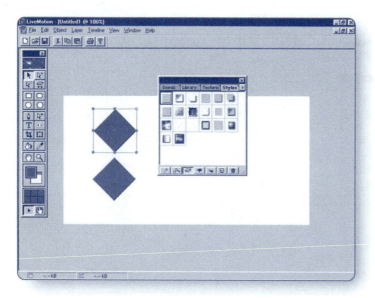

• **View Styles with Object Layers** shows the styles that have multiple layers. After you apply these styles, you can deconstruct them by using the Object Layers palette and easily make changes to the style you have added.

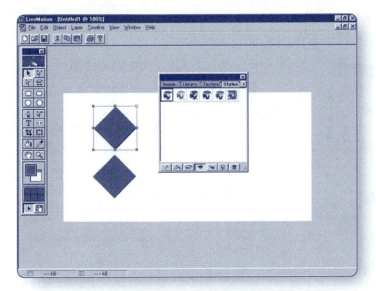

• **View Styles with Photoshop Filters** displays the styles that have special Photoshop effects that can be applied to images.

> **NOTE**
>
> If you have all the styles displayed, you may need to deselect some of them. In this case, click the view buttons of the styles you do *not* want to include, leaving only the type you want to see selected.

Applying a Style

Applying a style in LiveMotion is as simple as finding a style you want and trying it out. If you attempt to add a style and then find that you don't like it, remember to use the almost unlimited Undo options, available in the Edit menu.

Adding a Style to Create a Simple Button

When is a shape not a shape? When it's a button. LiveMotion enables you to turn flat, ordinary shapes into something special. To enhance a shape and turn it quickly into a Web-ready button, follow these steps:

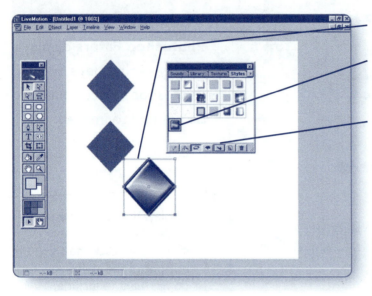

1. Select the object.

2. Click on the style you want to use for the button.

3. Click on the Apply Style button. The Style you selected is added to the object.

NOTE

If you want to apply a style quickly, you can simply select the style you want to use and drag it over an object. When you release it, the style is applied to the object.

Adding Styles to Text

Effects can be also added to any text you create in LiveMotion. You can choose from high-color and subtle shadows to dramatic, swirling effects and animation techniques.

NOTE

LiveMotion treats graphic objects, geometric shapes, and text objects similarly. You can apply styles, animation, and rollover effects to text in the same way you apply them to other objects.

1. Click on the Text tool and then create your text as usual.

> **NOTE**
>
> For more information on working with text objects in LiveMotion, see Chapter 7, "Working with Text in LiveMotion."

2. Click on the text object to select it. Object handles will appear around the object.

3. Open the Styles palette by choosing Styles from the Window menu (or press F10).

4. Click on the style you want to use.

5. Click on the Apply Style button. The text is displayed in the style you selected.

Applying Styles to Multiple Objects

As simple as this is, it's not much harder to apply the same style to many objects at once. Suppose that you've just created an object that is a combination of a number of Library shapes. You can apply a uniform style to them all at the same time.

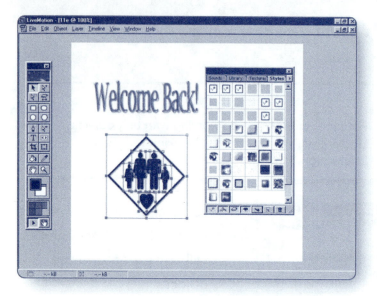

Here's how:

1. Create the objects you want to use.

2. Position the objects as you want them.

NOTE

The LiveMotion Library provides a wide range of ready-made objects you can include in your own compositions. For more about using the LiveMotion Library, see Chapter 10.

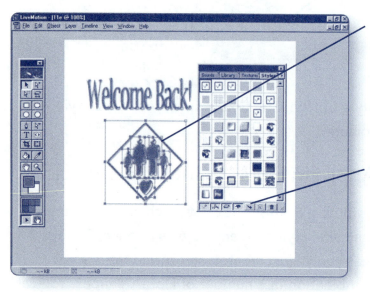

3. Select all objects using the selection tool.

4. Click the style you want to apply to the group.

5. Click Apply Style. The entire group is placed in the style you selected.

Modifying Styles

Although LiveMotion includes a fairly healthy selection of graphical, animation, and rollover styles, you will definitely want to add to the collection as your experience with the program continues. You can easily modify existing styles and add them to the Styles palette; or you can create your own from scratch. Either way, you can easily modify LiveMotion styles and then preserve those changed styles to use again in later projects.

Copying Styles

When you copy an object in LiveMotion, you pick up all of the object's attributes. When you paste a style, however, you choose specifically to paste only the style attribute from the object. Here are the steps:

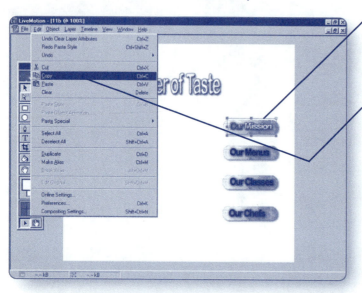

1. Select the object that contains the style you want to copy.

2. Choose Copy from the Edit menu (or press Ctrl+C for Windows or Cmd+C for Mac).

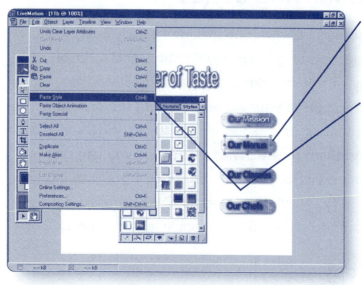

3. Select the object to which you want to apply the style.

4. Click Edit and choose Paste Style (or press Ctrl+B for Windows or Cmd+B for Mac). The copied style is applied to the selected object.

NOTE

LiveMotion does not save sounds attached to an object as part of a saved style in the Styles palette.

Changing Styles

In Chapter 8, "Creating and Using Layers," you learned about working with layers to make modifications to different levels of your objects. When you change styles you've created or adopted from the palette, you may need to divide the object into layers in order to see which items you want to change. The process is straightforward:

1. Select the object with which you want to work.

2. Display the Layers palette and choose the layer you want to change.

3. Open other palettes as needed (such as the Color palette shown here) to make the necessary change.

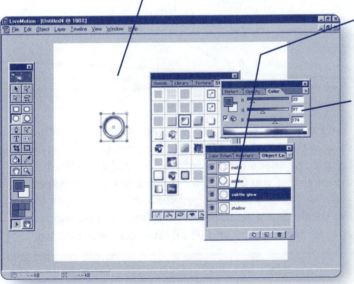

Saving a Changed Style

Once you make a few changes to a style, you may decide you want to keep it. LiveMotion makes it easy for you. Simply drag the style to the Styles palette. The Name dialog box opens.

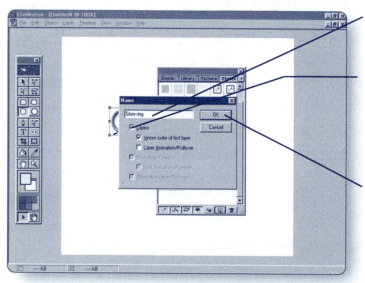

1. Type a name for the new style.

2. If you want to save the layers as well, verify that the Layers checkbox is checked.

3. Click on OK. The style is saved to the Styles palette.

NOTE

Don't see the style you just created? When LiveMotion saves a style to the palette, the program puts the style back in the shape of the rectangular image shown. This means that if you created a diamond or circular shape, you may not see the changed style at first. But look for the subtle or not-so-subtle style differences you added instead of the shape and you'll find your new creation.

Removing Styles

There may be those styles you think are plain
duds—ones you aren't likely to use again. You
should delete them so they don't take up room in
the Styles palette. Follow these steps to remove
styles you no longer need or want:

1. Click the style in the Styles palette you want to
delete.

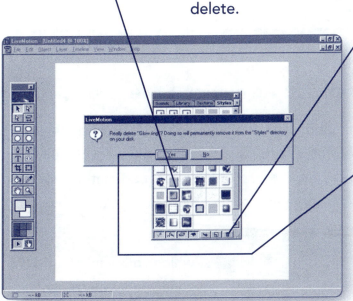

2. Click on the Remove
Style button. A warning
box appears, asking
whether you want to
continue.

3. Click on Yes to delete
the style.

> **NOTE**
>
> Remember that once a
> style is deleted from the
> Styles palette, it cannot
> be recovered.

Creating New Styles

The task of creating your own styles is as simple as
creating an image or text style you like and saving

it to the Styles palette. But you can also create new styles from combinations of existing ones by mixing and matching color, shadow, rollover, and animation styles.

NOTE

You can also create new styles while working in the Timeline window. To find out more about saving motion styles to the Styles palette, see Chapter 15, "Creating Animations."

Applying Animation Styles

Animations are fun, whether you're using the ones LiveMotion provides or creating them yourself. You can easily add one of the preset animation styles from the palette to an object in your composition.

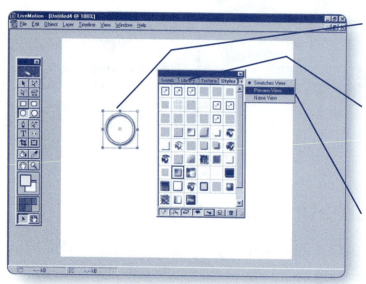

1. Select the object to which you want to add the style.

2. From the Window menu, choose Styles to open the Styles palette, if necessary.

3. Click the arrow to the right of the Styles tab and choose Preview View from the submenu.

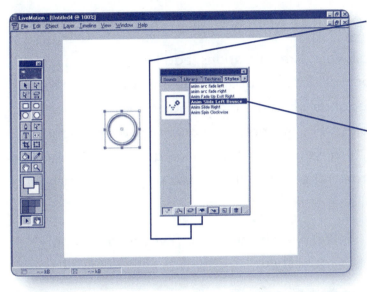

4. Deselect the other view buttons so that only animation styles are displayed.

5. Select the animation you want to use and click Apply Style. The style with animation is applied to your object.

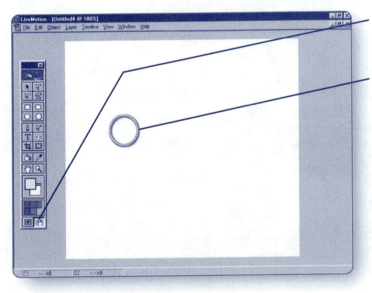

6. Click on the Preview Mode button.

7. The object moves through the animation.

NOTE

If you decide that you want to apply a rollover rather than an animation style, undo the animated sequence. From the Edit menu, choose Undo Apply Style to return the object to its pre-animation form.

Applying Rollover Styles

Rollovers, like animations, add life to your compositions. A rollover is like a *hot* button that responds when the mouse pointer passes over the object. For example, you might have text highlight or turn; you might flash an image or flip a picture as a rollover effect. Here are the steps for applying a rollover style:

1. Select the object to which you want to apply the rollover style.

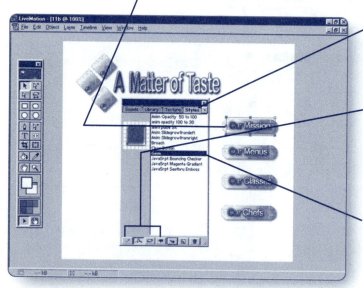

2. From the Window menu, choose Styles to open the Styles palette.

3. Deselect the view buttons so that only rollover styles are displayed.

4. Select the rollover style you want to apply.

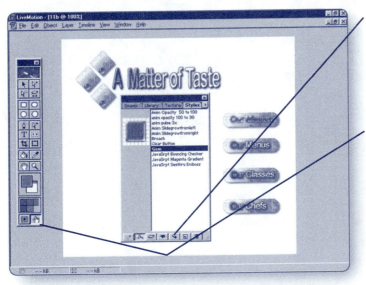

5. Click on the Apply Style button. The rollover is now applied to your object.

6. Click on the Select Preview Mode button to see how the rollover will work in your composition.

A Quick Summary

In this chapter, you've learned how to apply easy and cool effects to LiveMotion objects using the Styles palette. With styles that include basic design enhancements, plus animation, rollover, and Photoshop filters, you already have a good selection of special effects for use in your compositions. Specifically, this chapter discussed how to display styles in LiveMotion and select, apply, modify, and save styles. Additionally, you learned to work with styles that have built-in animation and rollover effects. The next chapter takes you into the 3-D realm by exploring special effects in LiveMotion.

12

Working with Special Effects

LiveMotion makes it easy for you to turn ordinary logos, images, shapes, and text into attention-getting designs and animations. By applying LiveMotion's special effects, either to a static image or as part of an animation, you can give objects shape, texture, and unique looks that make your compositions memorable. In this chapter, you will learn to

- Apply 3D effects.
- Add distortion to objects.
- Change layer and object textures.

Applying 3D Effects

Adding a 3D effect gives your objects depth and lighting features, making them appear to "stand out" from the screen display. Use the 3D palette, available in the Window menu, to apply 3D effects.

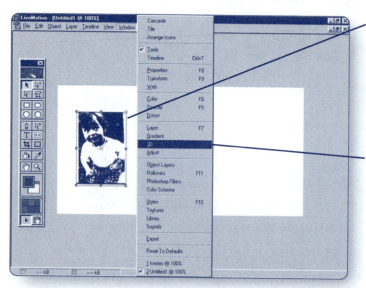

1. Click on (select) the object to which you want to apply the 3D effect. Handles appear around the object.

2. From the Window menu, choose 3D. The 3D palette opens.

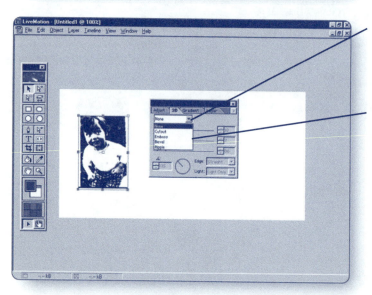

3. Click on the 3D Effect drop-down arrow. The list of 3D choices appears.

4. Click on your choice from the displayed list.

• **Cutout** makes the selected object appear to be set back into the surrounding area.

• **Emboss** causes the object to stand out, with highlighting, from the rest of the object.

• **Bevel** creates a plateau effect with side edges.

• **Ripple** creates a wavered effect in which light is reflected off a rippled surface.

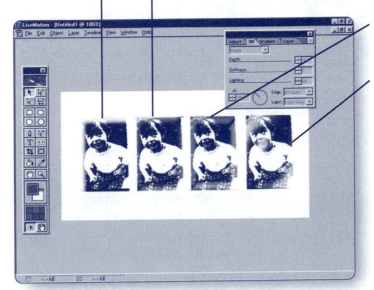

Changing 3D Depth and Softness

Once you choose the 3D effect you want to use, you can further control the way in which the effect is applied. By changing the *depth* of the effect, you change the way in which the object is offset from its shadow or highlight effect; by changing the softness, you modify the sharpness of the edges of the object. To change the depth and softness settings, use these steps:

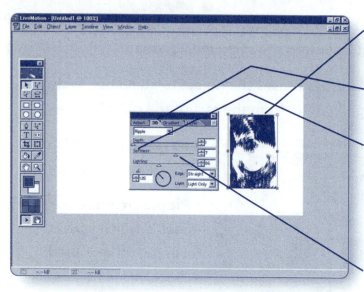

1. Select the object you want to change.

2. Open the 3D palette, if necessary.

3a. Drag the Depth slider to the left to decrease the depth of the effect.

OR

3b. Drag the Depth slider to the right to increase the effect.

TIP

Use the 3D lighting effect in an animation to rotate the display of lighting around an object or add a sudden flash to one area of an object.

Modifying Lighting of 3D Effects

One of the key elements in creating an impressive 3D effect is determining the way in which light is reflected off the object. LiveMotion enables you to control the intensity of the light, as well as the direction from which it comes and the overall balance of light and dark reflection.

To change the light intensity of an object, use the Lighting control in the 3D palette. Here's how:

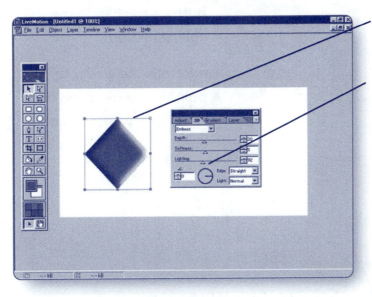

1. Select the object with which you want to work.

2. Drag the Lighting slider to the left to decrease the intensity of lighting or to the right to increase the light intensity.

> **NOTE**
>
> You can also enter a numeric value in the Lighting text box, or use the increase or decrease buttons to specify a particular lighting value.

Controlling Light Source

To change the way in which light is reflected off an object, use the angle settings or the lighting wheel. Use one of these methods to change the direction of the light source:

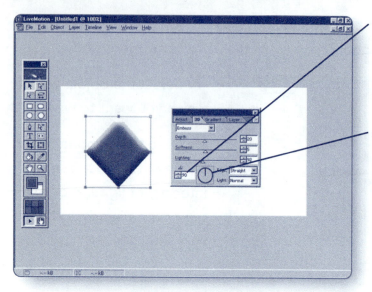

• Click on the Angle increase or decrease buttons to change the light direction.

• Rotate the wheel to point in the direction from which you want the light to come.

Selecting Light and Dark Balance

You can also change the balance of light and dark shading used to highlight the object you've selected. This control is available in the Light box in the 3D palette, if you've selected a 3D effect for your object. Here are the steps:

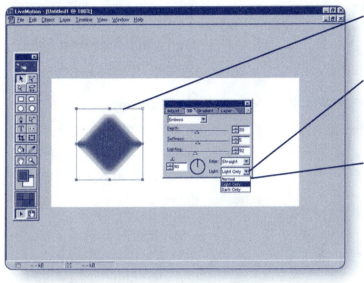

1. Select the object with which you want to work.

2. Click on the Light drop-down arrow and select the effect you want.

• Normal is the default, which displays equal light and dark values.

• Light Only displays only light reflection in the object; no dark shadowing is displayed.

• Dark Only displays only dark reflection in the object; no light reflection is displayed.

NOTE

For a realistic 3D effect, you need both light and dark highlights (which is created with the Normal selection). For special effects, however, you may want to experiment with Light Only and Dark Only values.

Selecting Edge Settings for 3D Objects

Another way in which you can modify the look of a 3D object is by changing the appearance of the edge of the object. The look you create will vary depending on the edge you select. To make the change, follow these steps:

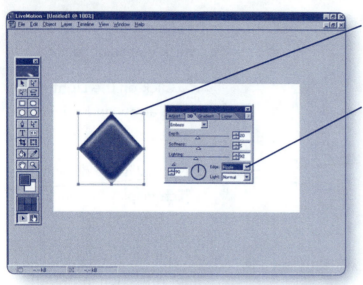

1. Select the object you want to change and display the 3D palette.

2. Click on the Edge drop-down arrow. A list of Edge effects appears so that you can make your choice:

• Straight leaves the edges of the object straight (this is the default value).

• Button creates a rounded and highlighted edge, making the edge stand out from the display.

• Plateau creates a raised surface, also reinforcing the idea that the object is standing away from the screen.

• Ripple creates a special edge effect that creates a small curve just inside the edge of the object, implying something that is impressed into and rises above the flat surface of the screen.

Adding Distortion

By adding the distortion effect to your objects and images, you can further modify your compositions. Distortion may blur, digitize, swirl, or displace the object, giving it a special—and memorable—look.

Begin using the distortion effect by opening the
Distort palette.

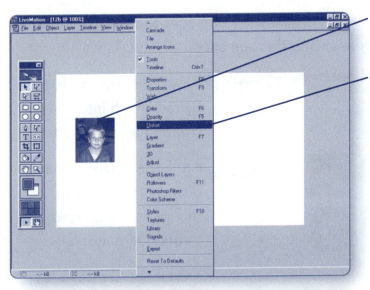

1. Select the object you
want to work with.

2. From the Window
menu, choose Distort.

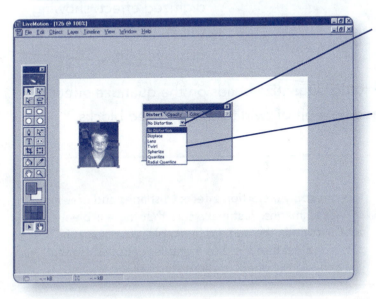

3. Click on the Distort
drop-down arrow. A list of
distortion choices appears.

4. Select the distortion
effect you want. Your
choices are as follows:

• Displace enables you to move the image or object within the object area, creating an off-center effect.

• Lens magnifies the object as though the viewer were seeing through a lens.

• Twirl distorts the image by rotating it internally, creating a twisted effect.

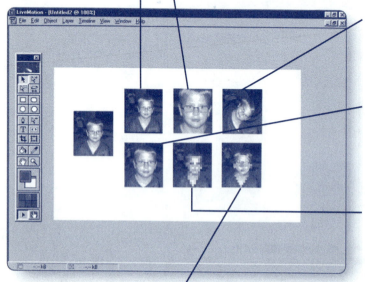

• Spherize magnifies and distorts the image as though it is displayed through a rounded lens.

• Quantize creates a digitized effect, showing the image blocked into displayed bits.

• Radial Quantize builds on the quantize effect by adding a bit of twirl to the digitized blocks.

NOTE

You can apply distortion effects to shapes and drawings as well as images. Just make sure that there is plenty of contrast within the item (for example, your object is patterned, textured, or has a gradient applied) so that you can see the effect of the distortion.

Displacing Images

When you opt to apply the Displace effect to your distorted image, you can control the amount of space by which the image is offset from its boundary. Additionally, you can decide how much you want to magnify the image as you distort it. Here are the steps for making these changes:

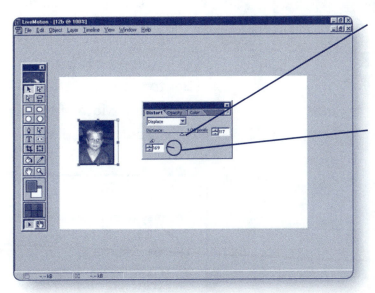

1. Drag the Distance slider to change the position of the image within the object.

2. Drag the wheel or click on the Angle arrows to change the angle at which the image is displayed.

NOTE

The Magnification option in Lens and Spherize distortion options enables you to control how large the image is in the displayed layer.

Twirling Images

Using the Twirl distortion effect, you can create the effect of movement in your animations. Twirl gives you two primary options to change: Turns and Band Size.

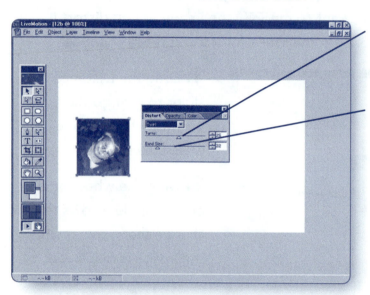

1. Use the Turns slider to control how far your object turns.

2. Drag the Band Size slider to the right to increase the width of the bands used in the spin.

TIP

You may want to use the Twirl effect, for example, in a rollover animation in which you spin an image on a button.

Changing Textures

Another way in which you can add special effects to your LiveMotion objects is to add textures to a selected layer. LiveMotion comes with a number of preset textures, and you can add your own from other sources as well. Here are the steps for applying a texture:

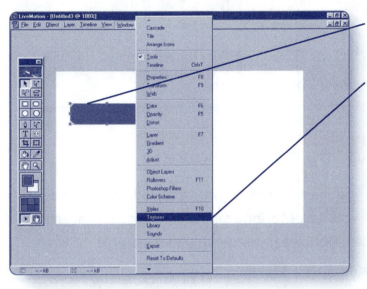

1. Click on the object with which you want to work.

2. From the Window menu, choose Textures. The Textures palette will open.

Applying a Texture

To apply a texture to an object or object layer, follow these steps:

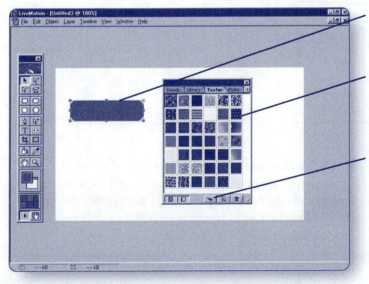

1. Click on the object you are modifying.

2. Click on the texture in the Textures palette you want to use.

3. Click on the Apply Texture button. The texture is added to the selected object.

TIP

Undo a texture application you just made by choosing Edit, Undo Apply Texture, or by pressing Ctrl+Z (Windows) or Cmd+Z (Mac).

Adding a New Texture

If you have an image you want to use as a texture in your LiveMotion composition, you can add it to the Texture palette. Follow these steps:

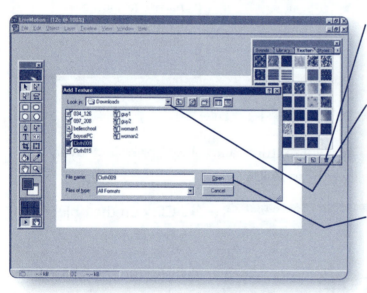

1. Click on the New Texture button in the Textures palette.

2. In the Add Texture dialog box, navigate to the drive and folder storing the file you want to use.

3. Click on Open. The texture is added to the palette.

NOTE

To remove textures you no longer need, click on the texture in the palette and then click on the Delete Texture button. A warning message will appear, asking you whether you want to proceed with the deletion. Click on Yes to delete the texture.

A Quick Summary

In this chapter, you've learned how to add special effects to your LiveMotion compositions. A special effect can enhance a static object, or you can use it as part of an animation that grows from 2D to 3D and back again. Specifically, in this chapter, you've learned how to apply 3D effects to your documents, select and work with distortion effects, and change and add textures to your objects. The next chapter talks about an exciting technique you can use to merge what you've learned about creating, modifying, and enhancing LiveMotion objects: creating rollovers for your compositions.

13

Creating Rollover Techniques

Rollovers are one of LiveMotion's strong suits. The program makes it easy for you to create special Web effects that cause an object to "change" when the user passes the mouse over it. With LiveMotion, you can create simple rollovers such as changing a button from one color to another or complete animations that play in response to the mouse position. In this chapter, you will learn to

- Apply existing rollover effects.
- Create a simple rollover.
- Create a customized rollover.
- Link rollover effects.

Understanding Rollovers

By adding rollovers to the sites you create, you can create an interactive experience for your visitors. Rollovers create an action when the user passes the mouse over or clicks on an element that contains a rollover effect. That action might be

- A button that lights up or glows.

- Highlighting of a menu item.

- Selection of a table row or column.

- The appearance of a tool tip or description.

- An animation that plays or an image that displays.

Applying Existing Rollover Effects

You can add a rollover effect on-the-fly using one of LiveMotion's predesigned rollover effects. They're available in the Styles palette. To apply a predesigned rollover effect to an object, follow these steps:

1. Create the object to which you want to add the rollover effect.

NOTE

A rollover effect can be applied to any object you create in LiveMotion. Text, images, clip art, photographs, shapes, and custom drawings can all be given rollovers.

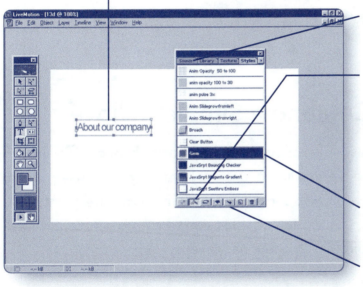

2. Open the Styles palette by pressing F10.

3. Deselect all view buttons except the Rollover button. You will now see only the styles with rollovers attached.

4. Click on the rollover style you want.

5. Click on the Apply Style button.

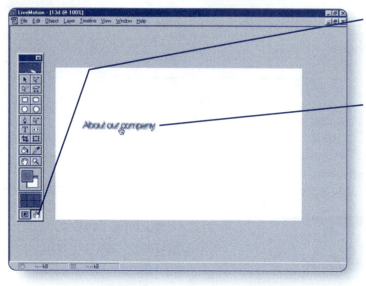

6. Preview the rollover by clicking on the Preview button

7. Roll the mouse pointer over the object to see the rollover event.

Creating a Simple Rollover

A simple rollover requires basically one thing: An object that looks one way before the mouse passed over it and another way when the mouse points to it. LiveMotion enables you to create simple rollovers in a few easy steps:

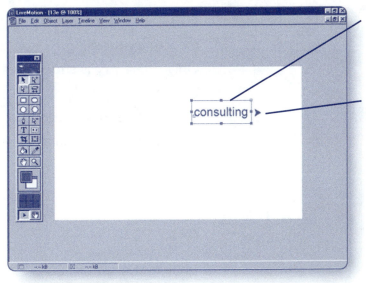

1. Create the button or other object to which you want to add the rollover.

2. Add shadow, color, and style treatment. (In this example, the text was enlarged and a blue-gray shade was applied.)

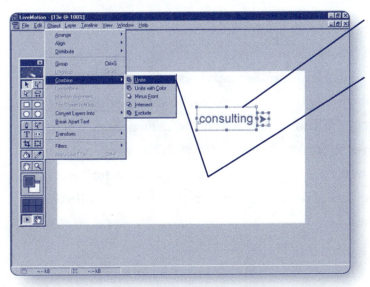

3. Select all items in your button or object.

4. From the Object menu, choose Combine, Unite. The objects are combined into a complete group.

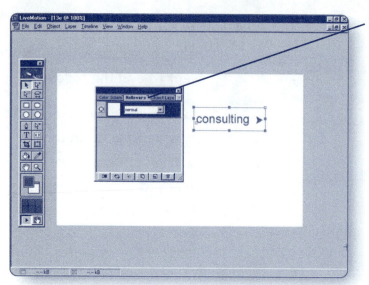

5. Open the Rollovers palette by pressing F11. Only one entry is shown in the palette by default; the Normal selection refers to the object in its regular state.

Checking Out the Rollovers Palette

The Rollovers palette contains everything you need to link rollover effects to your objects. Although you will use familiar palettes, such as Color, Style, Library, and Opacity, to make the changes that occur in the object when the user passes the mouse over it, you tell LiveMotion which changes to make when by applying those effects in the Rollover palette. These are the important items in this palette:

NOTE

Later in this chapter, you'll learn how to link rollover effects on multiple objects. For a simple rollover, the target button is not used.

• **Selected State.** The state that is currently selected is highlighted in the Rollovers palette. In each state, you see its name, thumbnail preview, and a target button that enables you to link rollover effects in multiple rollovers.

• **Edit Behaviors.** This button enables you to change the behaviors of a rollover effect.

NOTE

Behaviors are the way in which objects react when a specific event (like a rollover) is encountered. You'll learn more about object behaviors in Chapter 14 when timelines are discussed.

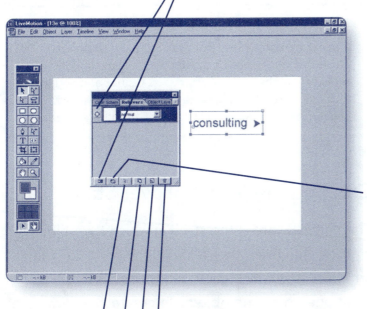

• **Replace Image.** The Replace Image button swaps one image for another in your composition.

• **Sound.** This button enables you to add a sound event to your rollover in the specified state.

• **Duplicate Rollover State.** Click this button to copy a selected rollover state.

• **New Rollover State.** Use this button to add a new rollover state.

• **Delete Rollover State.** Click this button to

remove the selected rollover state.

TIP

Once a rollover state performs exactly the way you want it to, using Duplicate Rollover State enables you to use the same effect again without re-creating it. You can then make any modifications you need to the object containing the "new" rollover state.

NOTE

Both Sound and Delete Rollover State are disabled (grayed) in this figure because thus far the example involves only the Normal state. You cannot add sound to or delete the Normal state. When you add a new rollover state, Sound and Delete will both be available.

Creating the New Rollover State

The normal state is the state in which the object is created. To create the rollover, you need to create an effect that will occur when the mouse pointer is positioned over the object. To create the new state:

1. Click on the New Rollover State button. The new state is created.

2. Click the drop-down arrow. You are given several options:

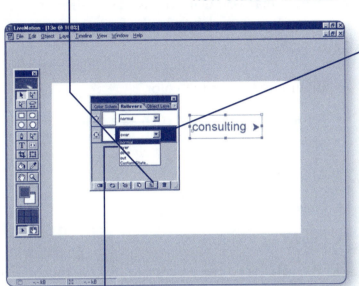

• **Normal** is the state in which the object is created.

• **Over** is the state triggered when the mouse is positioned over the object.

• **Down** is the state triggered when the mouse is clicked on the object.

• **Out** is the state applied when the mouse is moved off the object.

• **Custom state** is a state you create for actions other than the ones listed.

NOTE

Later in this chapter, in "Creating a Custom Rollover State," you'll learn how to create a custom state to link two objects with their own rollover effects.

---

3. Click on the Over option to create an action that is carried out when the user passes the mouse over the object.

Adding Rollover Effects

Now decide what you want the rollover effect to do when the mouse pointer passes over the object. Possible choices might be

- Changing the object color.
- Adding a visual effect such as a "glow" to the object.
- Animating the object.
- Playing a chime.
- Enlarging the object.

To add the effects to the new state, follow these steps:

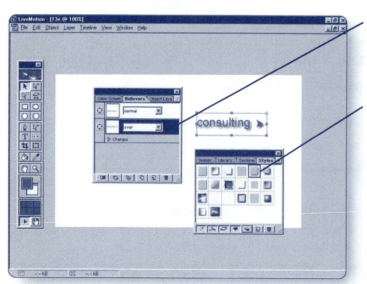

1. Select the rollover state to which you want to apply the changes.

2. Add the changes you want the rollover to perform.

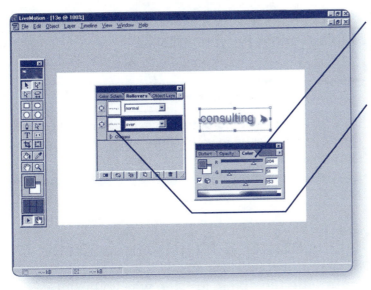

3. Another common change is modification of color.

4. The new effects are displayed in the rollover preview.

Checking Your Changes

LiveMotion keeps track of the changes you add to the rollover effect so that you can make further modifications if necessary. To review the changes you've made, follow these steps:

1. Verify that the object is selected.

2. In the Rollovers palette, click the Changes down arrow. A list of options appears.

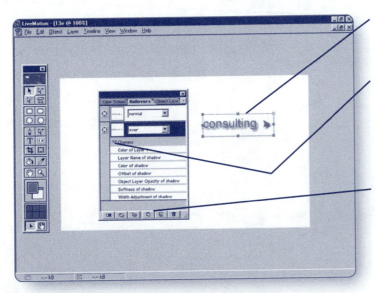

3. Drag the bottom border of the Rollovers

palette, if necessary, to see the complete list of possible changes for your rollover.

NOTE

If you find that you've forgotten something or want to make another change to your rollover effect, you can make changes or additions at any time.

Duplicating a Rollover State

Once you get an object just the way you want it, you can copy the effects. In this example, I wanted to return the color from magenta back to blue, but I also wanted to retain the drop shadow.

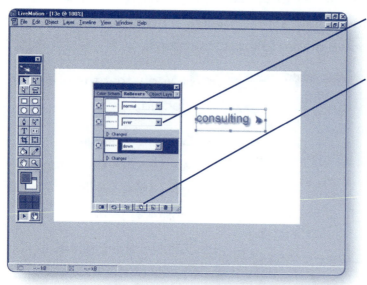

1. Select the rollover state you want to copy.

2. Click on the Duplicate Rollover State button. A rollover state is added to the list. The "down" state is selected by default.

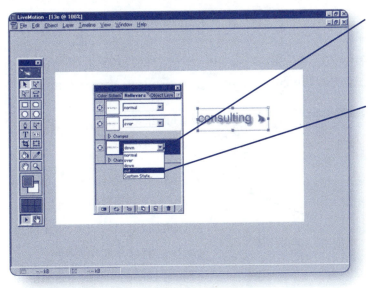

3. Click on the State drop-down arrow. The list of states is displayed.

4. Click on out. (This controls the object behavior when the pointer is moved off the object.)

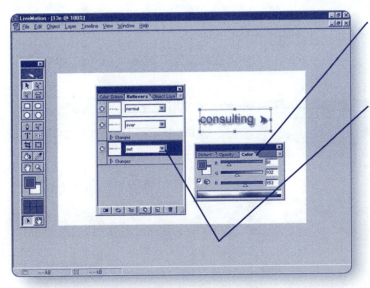

5. If necessary, open the Color palette by pressing F6.

6. To match the color values in the original color, click on normal; then click on out and use the same color values.

7. Save your work by pressing Ctrl+S (Windows) or Cmd+S (Mac).

Previewing Your Rollover

You can (and should) preview the rollover to see how it will work on your site. Follow these steps:

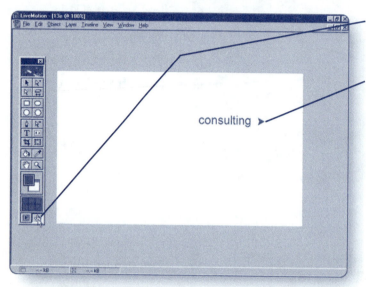

1. Click on the Preview Mode button.

2. Move the mouse pointer to the object. You should see the rollover states that you assigned. This example creates these effects:

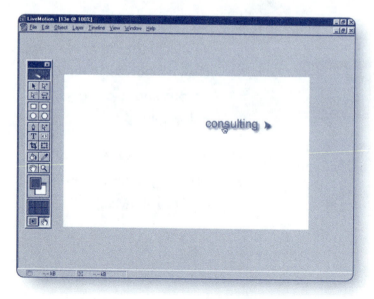

• When the mouse is placed on the object, the object changes to a magenta color with a drop shadow.

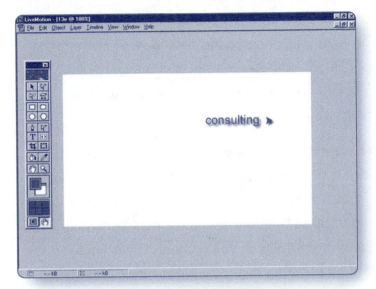

• When the mouse passes off of the object, the magenta changes back to blue but the shadow remains.

Troubleshooting Rollovers

My rollover didn't work! If your rollover effect didn't work, click on the object and reopen the Rollovers palette by pressing F11. Check the rollover states to make sure that you have assigned the changes you want to the Over effect. If you assigned the effects to Down instead of Over, your changes will occur only when you click the object.

It changed to the wrong color. If your rollover worked at the right time and in response to the right action but changed to the wrong color, simply click on the object, open the Rollovers palette by pressing F11, and review your settings. It could be that you applied the wrong color or you applied the correct color to a different state.

The effect worked only when I clicked on it. This is an example of choosing the "down" state rather than the Over state. Simply click on the object, press F11 to open the Rollovers palette, and change the state.

The object did something unexpected. Similarly, click on the object and open the Rollovers palette (F11). Click on the Changes drop-down arrow to review the settings. If you have previously assigned an animated style to your object, the animation may still be affecting the object. Undo the Style addition and then reset your rollover effects.

Creating Custom Rollovers

Another type of rollover you may want to add to your compositions is a bit more sophisticated. In this rollover, you use two objects—each with its own rollover effects. Passing the mouse pointer over or clicking on one object triggers an action in the other object. You might use this type of rollover, for example, to

- Display the photo of your staff when the user positions the pointer on "About us."

- Display a help box when a user hesitates over a menu choice.

- Play a quick animation in another part of the page when the user clicks on a button.

Creating the Trigger

The first object you'll create is called the *trigger* object because it triggers the response action in the second object. You might want to create a text object, for example, that is linked to an image. When the mouse passes over the text button, the image appears.

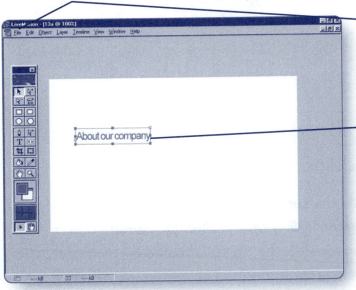

1. Start a new composition, if necessary, by choosing File, New and then clicking on OK.

2. Create your object and apply the styles you want for the beginning (or normal) state.

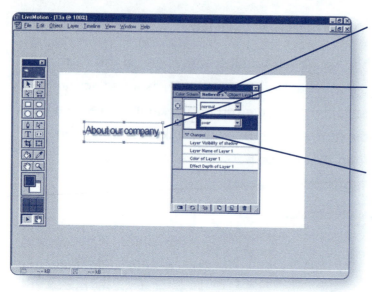

3. Open the Rollovers palette by pressing F11.

4. Create the rollover effect you want for the first object.

5. Display the changes to review your selections.

Adding the Remote Object

Add the second object that will be linked to the trigger. This is often called the *remote* object because it is the object affected by the action, not the one triggering the action. In this example, an image will be displayed as the remote object. Here are the steps:

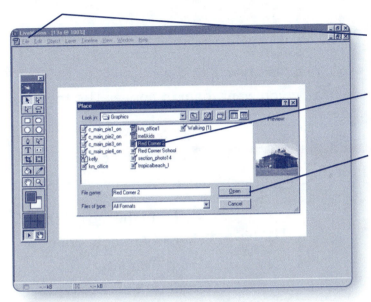

1. From the File menu, choose Place.

2. Select the file you want to place.

3. Click on Open. The file is placed in the composition.

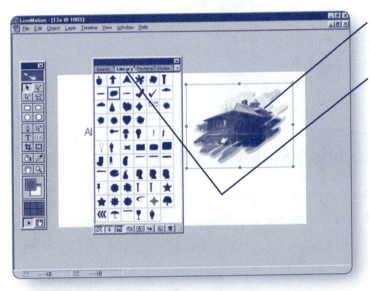

4. Make any modifications you want to the object.

5. This example applies a matte from the Library palette to the photograph.

Positioning the Objects

Next, move the objects to the place in the composition you want them to appear. Use these steps:

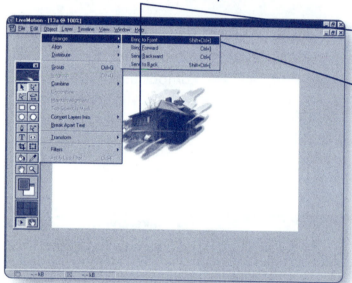

1. Drag the objects to their respective positions.

2. From the Object menu, choose Arrange, Bring to Front. This layers the objects (if necessary).

Creating Rollovers for the New Object

You also need to add the rollover to the new object. Here are the steps:

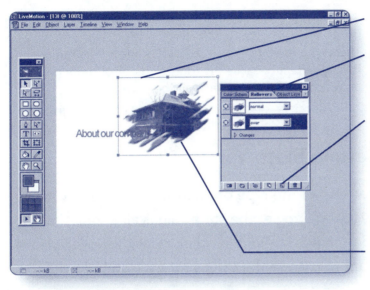

1. Select the new object.

2. Press F11 to open the Rollovers palette.

3. Click on the New Rollover State button. A new rollover state is added to the list. The state Over is selected by default.

4. Make any changes you want to add to the object.

Creating a Custom State

Next, you need to create the custom state that will enable you to link the rollover effects between objects. Here are the steps:

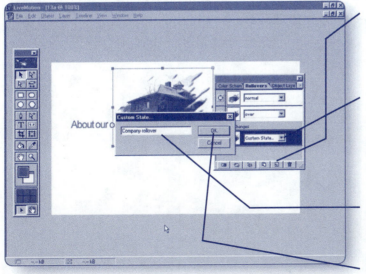

1. Click on the New Rollover State button. A new state is added.

2. Click on the state drop-down arrow and choose Custom State. The Custom State message box opens.

3. Type a name for the Custom state.

4. Click on OK. The state is added to the list in the Rollovers palette.

> **NOTE**
>
> There's no need to create an "out" state for the remote rollover effect because the triggering object is the one on which the mouse will actually be placed.

Setting State Values

Because of the type of rollover effect created here, it is simple to set the state values all at one time. To keep things straight in other cases, however, you'll want to choose the values for each state as they are created.

In this example, the image is invisible until the mouse pointer is passed over the trigger object, and then it appears. When the mouse pointer moves off the trigger, the image disappears. To make things appear and disappear, use the Objects tab in the Rollovers palette.

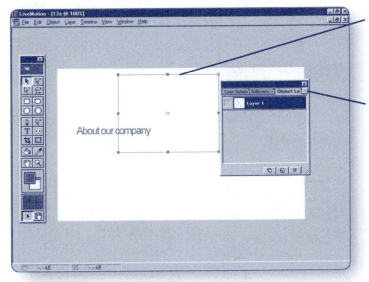

1. Verify that the object and the Normal rollover are both selected.

2. Click on the Object Layers tab. The Object Layers palette opens.

3. Click on the select box that appears at the far-left of Layer 1. This action hides the image.

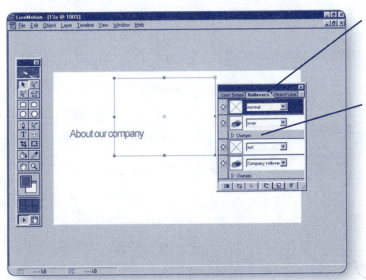

4. Click on the Rollovers tab. The Rollovers palette reopens.

5. Make any additional changes you need and then check your changes by clicking on the Changes drop-down arrow.

Linking the Objects with a Rollover

Now that you've added the rollovers you want for each of the objects, you need to link them so that the trigger object causes a remote response. Here are the steps:

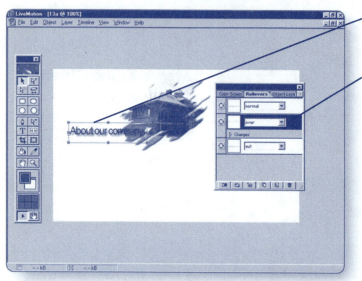

1. Click on the trigger object.

2. In the Rollovers palette, click on the state for the trigger when the other object is activated (in this case, Over).

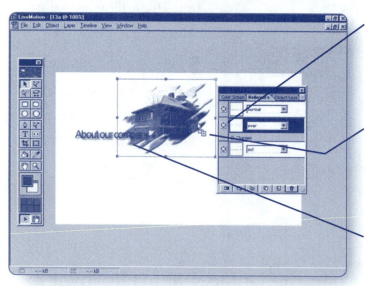

3. Position the mouse pointer on the small target symbol that appears to the left of the Over state.

4. Drag the target to the remote object. The pointer will include a special object pointer box.

5. Release the mouse button on the remote object. The link is established. This is what the Rollovers palette looks like when the trigger and remote object rollovers are linked:

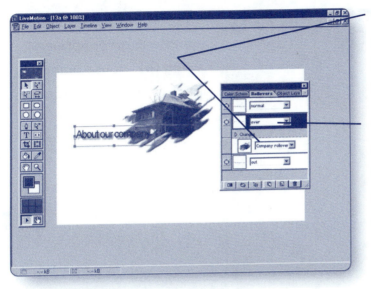

• The Custom State rollover is added to the Rollovers palette for the trigger object.

• The Over state is selected because this is the state during which the remote rollover is activated.

Previewing the Custom Rollover

Once your link is established, preview the effects you've created, using these steps:

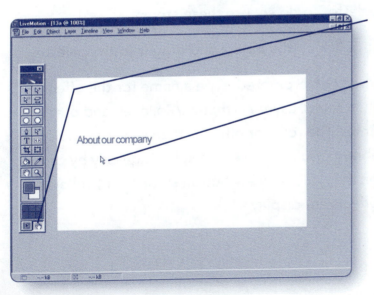

1. Click on the Preview button in the toolbox.

2. Place the mouse pointer on the trigger object. The remote object should respond in the way you specified.

• In this example, the remote rollover appears when the mouse pointer passes over the trigger object.

Save Your Rollover

Once the rollover is just the way you want it, save the effect you created by placing it in the Style palette. To do so, use these steps:

1. Click on the object and drag it to the palette.

2. When prompted, type a name for the effect, then select Layer Animation/Rollover, and press Enter. The rollover effect is then saved to the style library. You'll be able to display it quickly by clicking on the Rollover view button so that only rollover effects are displayed.

A Quick Summary

In this chapter, you've learned about one of the key interactive features LiveMotion offers: rollover effects. Rollovers enable you to add life and movement to your designs and give visitors something to hold their interest and navigate more easily through your site. Specifically, in this chapter, you learned to create, enhance, and preview both simple and custom rollovers. The next chapter takes this interactivity a step further by exploring the LiveMotion Timeline.

14

Working with the LiveMotion Timeline

LiveMotion excels at Web animations, and the Timeline is one of the primary tools you'll use in creating animations for your site. The Timeline enables you to create, sequence, and time the events that make your objects move. Specifically, in this chapter, you'll learn how to do the following:

- Display the Timeline.
- Understand Timeline elements.
- Work with objects on the Timeline.
- Work with keyframes.
- Create time-independent groups.
- Change the Timeline display.

What Will You Animate?

You might want to create an animation for your company's banner ad, or perhaps you want to swirl and twirl a company logo at the top of your site. Your only limitations on the types of animations you create are the limitations of your own imagination. In Chapter 15, "Creating Animations," you learn how to plan and create animations for your site. In this chapter, you learn how to use the Timeline window, which is a prerequisite for creating animations.

Displaying the Timeline

The first step in exploring the Timeline is displaying it. Begin with these steps:

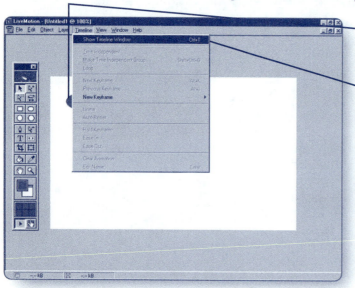

1. Create a new object or open an existing one.

2. From the Timeline menu, choose Show Timeline Window. The Timeline window opens.

TIP

You may want to close the toolbox so that it won't appear over the Timeline window. When you want to reopen it, open the Windows menu and choose Tools.

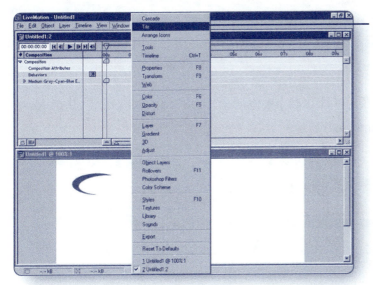

3. From the Window menu, choose Tile. LiveMotion tiles the Timeline and the composition window so that you can see both views as you work.

Understanding Timeline Elements

Timeline gives you the means to add, control, and orchestrate the events in your animations. The Timeline window includes the following important elements:

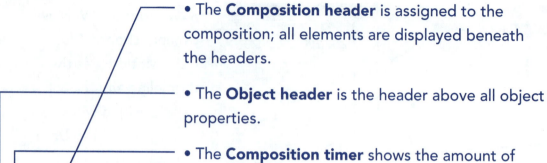

• The **Composition header** is assigned to the composition; all elements are displayed beneath the headers.

• The **Object header** is the header above all object properties.

• The **Composition timer** shows the amount of time elapsed from the beginning of playback.

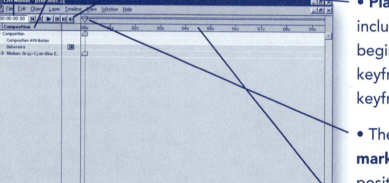

• **Playback controls** include rewind to beginning, previous keyframe, play, next keyframe, last keyframe.

• The **Current time marker** shows the current position on the Timeline.

• The **Timeline** displays the time intervals along which you place events.

NOTE

Timeline displays time movement using these increments: The "s" is seconds; "f" is frames.

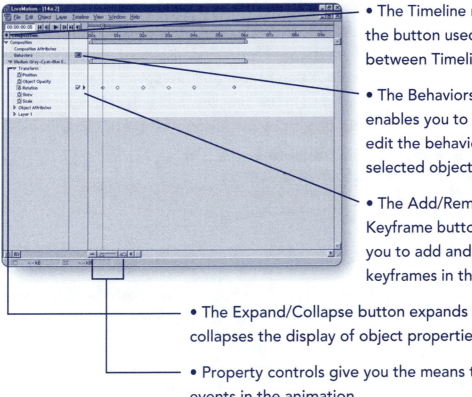

• The Timeline navigator is the button used to move between Timelines.

• The Behaviors button enables you to add and edit the behaviors of the selected object.

• The Add/Remove Keyframe button enables you to add and delete keyframes in the Timeline.

• The Expand/Collapse button expands and collapses the display of object properties.

• Property controls give you the means to change events in the animation.

• Zoom controls expand and/or reduce the increments on the Timeline.

TIP

The frame rate is set when you first create a new composition. You can edit the frame rate (12 per second) by choosing Edit, Composition Settings, and choosing a different rate in the dialog box.

Displaying Object Properties

When the Timeline is first displayed, the Composition header and the object headers are displayed in the Timeline. Make the changes to your objects by modifying the object's properties.

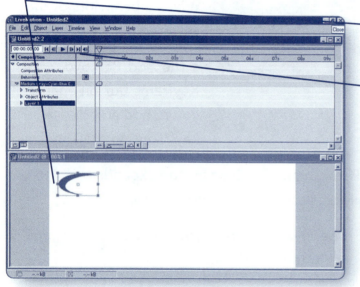

1. Select the object you want to animate.

2. Display the Timeline by pressing Ctrl+T (Windows users) or Cmd+T (Mac users). Both the object and the composition items are displayed. If necessary, resize the Timeline window so that you can view both the Timeline and the Composition window at the same time.

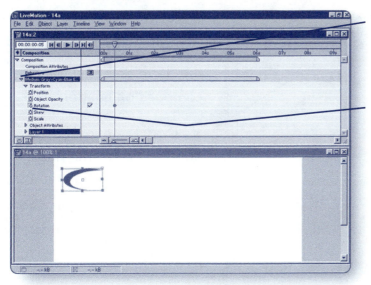

3. Click on the drop-down arrow to display the object properties.

4. Click on the stopwatch beside the Rotation property to activate the property and set a keyframe.

Setting Composition and Object Duration

Before you begin to add animation elements to your composition, you need to determine the overall duration of the composition and the length of time for each of the individual objects within the composition.

Choosing Composition Duration

To set the duration for the entire composition,

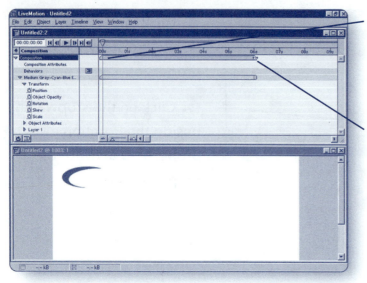

1. Position the mouse pointer on the left end of the duration bar in the composition header.

2. Drag the end of the duration bar to the right. As you extend the composition duration, the object duration extends automatically.

NOTE

You can also create time-independent objects within the composition. Time-independent objects or object groups have their own Timelines.

Changing Object Duration

To change the duration of the object within the composition—so that it appears after the start of the composition or ends before the finish, or both—you'll want to change the duration of the object.

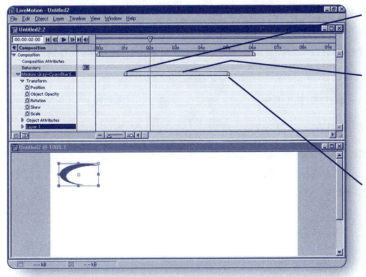

1. Point to the beginning marker of duration bar.

2. Drag the beginning marker to the right, measuring against the Timeline.

3. Drag the stop marker to the left, measuring against the Timeline.

TIP

If you want to move the entire object duration, you can simply click in the middle of the duration bar and drag the bar to the right or left.

Durations and More

How long do you want to allow for:

A rolling image in a banner ad? 2-3 seconds

A fluttering butterfly? 3-6 frames

A rotating logo? 2-4 seconds

A morphing animation? Total time, 2-4 seconds

Working with the Current Time Marker

The current time marker specifies where in the animation Timeline you are currently working. Drag the current time marker to the point on the Timeline where you want to add keyframes.

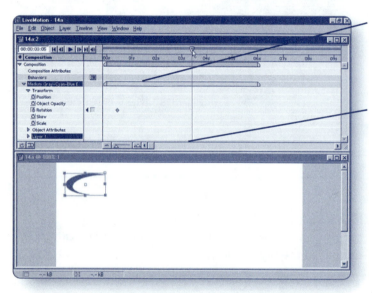

1. Decide where in the time sequence you want an event to occur.

2. Drag the current time marker to the new location.

Table 14.1. Moving the Current Time Marker

To move the marker	Quick Keys (Windows & Mac)
Beginning of composition	Home
End of composition	End
Back one frame	Page Up
Forward one frame	Page Down
Back 10 Frames	Shift+Page Up
Forward 10 Frames	Shift+Page Down

Working with Keyframes

A keyframe is a point on the Timeline that specifies a change in behavior. If you want to rotate an object, for example, you create keyframes at the points at which you turn the object. If you want to create an object that fades out of sight, you can decrease the opacity gradually by setting a series of keyframes and decreasing the opacity at each point.

Creating a Keyframe

Creating a keyframe involves two steps: determining where in the Timeline you want the change to occur; and selecting the property you want the change to affect. Here are the steps for creating a keyframe:

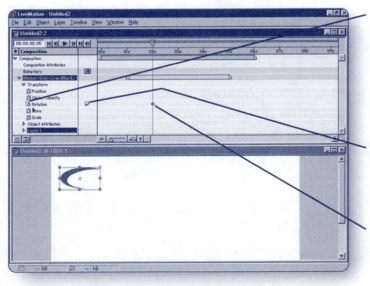

Click the property stopwatch to the left of the property you want to change. You'll see two immediate changes:

• The Add/Remove Keyframe checkbox appears.

• A keyframe is added in the selected behavior line at the current time marker.

Now you've created the first keyframe, but it's only a starting point. You need to add more keyframes in order to create the action.

Adding More Keyframes

The secret of the animation is in the way the object changes over time. This means you need to set additional keyframes to show a change in behavior.

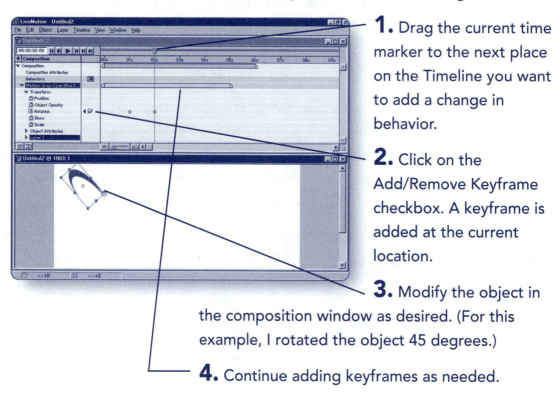

1. Drag the current time marker to the next place on the Timeline you want to add a change in behavior.

2. Click on the Add/Remove Keyframe checkbox. A keyframe is added at the current location.

3. Modify the object in the composition window as desired. (For this example, I rotated the object 45 degrees.)

4. Continue adding keyframes as needed.

Table 14.2. Keyframe Quick Keys

If you want to do this:	Press this combination (Windows)	Or this combination (Mac)
Move to the next keyframe	Alt+K	Opt+K
Move to the previous keyframe	Alt+J	Opt+J
Add Anchor Keyframe	Alt+Shift+A	Opt+Shift+AZ
Add Opacity Keyframe	Alt+Shift+T	Opt+Shift+T
Add Position Keyframe	Alt+Shift+P	Opt+Shift+P
Add Rotation Keyframe	Alt+Shift+R	Opt+Shift+R
Add Scale Keyframe	Alt+Shift+S	Opt+Shift+S

Testing Your Changes

You can view the changes you're making by taking a test run at playing the developing animation.

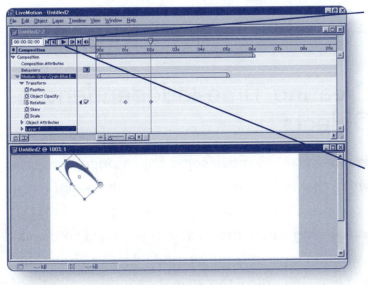

1. Click on the Rewind to Beginning button in the playback controls. The current time marker moves to the beginning of the Timeline.

2. Click on the Play button. LiveMotion plays your animation. (In this example, the object rotates a full circle in place.)

Moving Keyframes

After you add keyframes on the Timeline, you may want to fine-tune the action in your animation by moving them around.

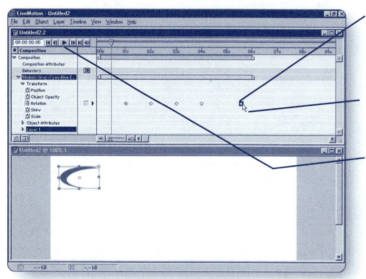

1. Click on the keyframe you want to move. The keyframe is highlighted.

2. Drag the keyframe to the new location.

3. Test the change by clicking Play.

NOTE

Delete a keyframe by clicking on the keyframe and then pressing the Delete button.

Creating Time-Independent Objects

You may want to move some objects independently within the animation. For example, you might have a composition that displays a running line of text announcing a new product, and you want to display a rotating logo at three-second intervals above the text line. To control the animation independently of the composition, you can make the object a time-independent object. Here's how:

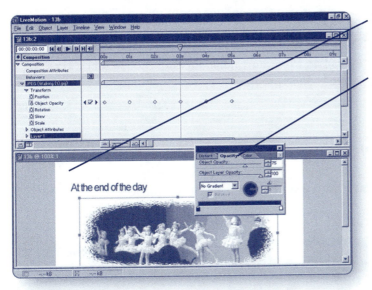

1. Open your composition.

2. Set the keyframes you want using the effects you choose (I used opacity to make an image gradually appear and disappear, but you might change color, rotate an object, or add some other change).

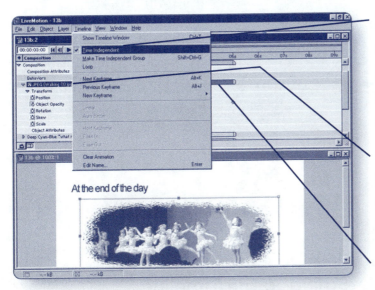

3. From the Timeline menu, choose Time Independent. The Timeline window displays these changes:

• A special time-independent icon appears to the left of the object header.

• The duration bar for that object appears grayed.

NOTE

In addition to creating independent object animations, you can create time-independent groups. To do this, select the group in your composition and then press Ctrl+Shift+G (Windows users), Cmd+Shift+G (Mac users), or, from the Timeline menu, choose Make Time Independent Group.

Working with Different Timelines

You can move to the time-independent Timeline for the selected object by following these steps:

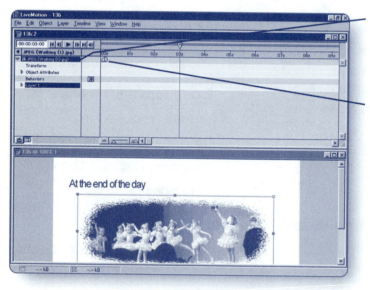

1. Double-click the object to open its independent time window.

2. Set the object duration by dragging the stop marker to the right on the behavior Timeline.

Setting Object Properties and Returning to the Timeline

Notice that the object displayed in the Time Independent Timeline has different properties available.

1. Select the object properties as desired.

2. Rewind and then play the animation to preview the independent action.

3. Click on the Timeline Selector button to return to the main Timeline window.

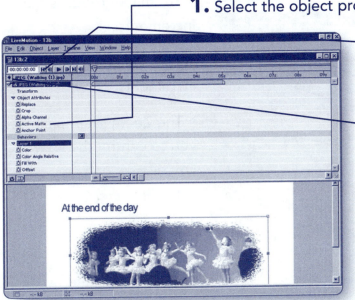

TIP

Your animation can be played by pressing the spacebar on either Windows or Mac systems.

Changing the Timeline Display

You can control the way in which the Timeline is displayed by using the Zoom controls. Why change the view? You might want to control the object animation by adding keyframes at close and measured intervals. Or perhaps you want to set your keyframes further apart for a slow change. The Timeline window offers you three zoom controls:

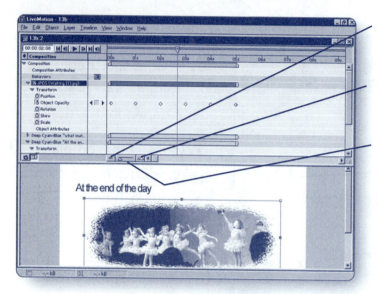

• Zoom Out reduces the increments.

• Zoom In enlarges the increments.

• The Zoom slider enables you to control the view you display.

Shrinking Time Increments

When you shrink the view on the Timeline, the frames are collapsed and you see only the seconds measurement. You may want to work in this view when you want to create and modify behaviors that play over several seconds.

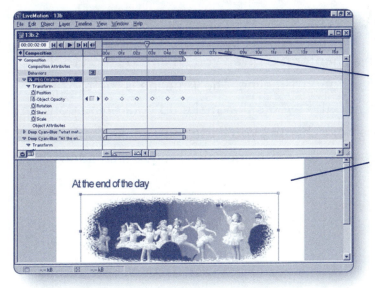

As you repeatedly click on the Zoom Out control:

• The display on the Timeline shrinks, showing only second increments.

• The composition window is not changed.

Expanding Time Increments

When you expand the view on the Timeline, the increments display frames as well as seconds. Here are the steps to change the display:

1. Click on the Zoom In control.

2. The Timeline view expands so that you can work with individual frames in the composition.

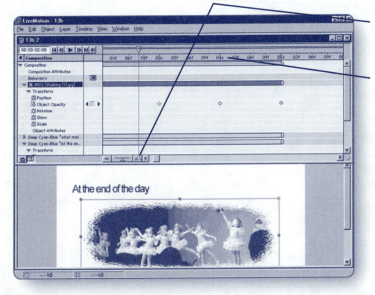

A Quick Summary

This chapter has given you an introduction to the LiveMotion Timeline. The Timeline is the tool used to add the events that make up your animations. In the next chapter, you'll use the Timeline and other features to create your own unique animations.

15

Creating Animations

In the preceding chapter, you learned about the LiveMotion Timeline. Specifically, you discovered how to view your composition elements, set duration, and change the Timeline view. You also learned a little bit about adding keyframes to signify an event in the animation you're creating. In this chapter, you build on your knowledge of the Timeline by learning how to use it to:

- Compose a simple animation.
- Create a looping animation.
- Add a behavior.
- Create custom behaviors.

Composing a Simple Animation

An animation can be as simple as a shape that rotates or as complex as a cartoon sequence. An animation is simply any object that moves. So whether a few letters jiggle in place or a complicated sequence of movies and interactive prompts occurs, LiveMotion gives you the tools to pull it all together smoothly and professionally.

Mapping Out the Animation

Animation all begins with you. Before you start creating your animation sequence on-screen, sketch it out on paper. Think about the following:

- **How long you want the animation to play.** Remember that longer animations take more time to download, and the average user will hang out at your site seven seconds or less before moving on in frustration. With animation, short is often sweet.

- **Whether it will be a single animation or it will contain other independent animated objects.** For example, you might run one animation sequence as an introduction and then display a series of four "snapshots" that appear one after another to familiarize your visitors with your key programs.

• **Where on the page you want the animation to occur.** To determine this, it's a good idea to actually map out the page. Sketch out the way you'd like the site to look. If you're working with a team, do it as a group, if possible.

Creating the Objects

You can animate existing objects, objects you create from the library, simple text, or groups of objects. Create the objects in the usual way, using the LiveMotion tools you've mastered thus far. Then, as you prepare to create your animation, follow these steps:

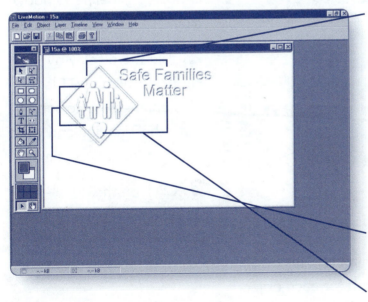

1. Create the object you want to animate. In this example, the object is a logo for a family service organization.

2. Determine the order in which you want to animate objects.

• Add colors to family members, left to right.

• Color the heart and program name last.

> **NOTE**
>
> Remember that any animation you create can easily be turned into a looping animation—that is, an animation that repeats automatically with no action from the visitor. This means that you can have continual motion on your site, if you choose, while keeping your animations small and your design simple.

Preparing the Display

Once you have the basic objects in place, you can begin working with them in the Timeline.

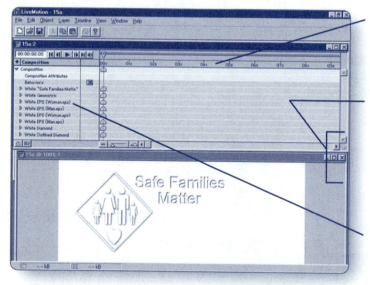

1. Open the Timeline by choosing Timeline Window from the Timeline menu.

2. Tile the display by choosing Window, Tile. This enables you to see both the Timeline and your composition at one time.

3. Click on the Expand/Collapse buttons for the objects you want to animate. This displays the properties you can work with for each object.

> **NOTE**
>
> If you need a refresher on setting object properties, see Chapter 14, "Working with the LiveMotion Timeline."

Setting Frame Rate

Before going any further, however, stop and think about the finished product. Determining the frame rate will impact you now in the way in which the Timeline itself is displayed. If you want to work at an average frame rate of 12 frames per second (the amount by default), your Timeline will be displayed initially in increments of seconds. As you enlarge the display (by using one of the zoom controls mentioned in Chapter 14), you will be able to work with individual frames.

When you first create a new composition, the Composition Settings dialog box is automatically opened. This is where you first determine the frame rate—the number of frames displayed per second in an animated sequence—you will use for your composition. You can go back and change the frame rate any time you choose. Here's how:

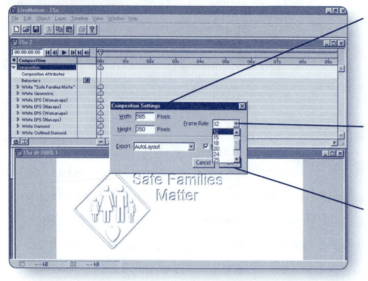

1. Open the Composition Settings dialog box by choosing Edit, Composition Settings.

2. Click on the Frame Rate drop-down arrow and select the rate you want.

3. Click on OK to return to the Timeline.

Setting Duration for Multi-Object Animations

The next step involves setting the duration of your composition and the individual animated objects. In the preceding chapter, you learned to set the duration for an entire composition and one object, but things get more complicated when you are working with multiple objects.

Consider, for example, the animations planned for this banner ad:

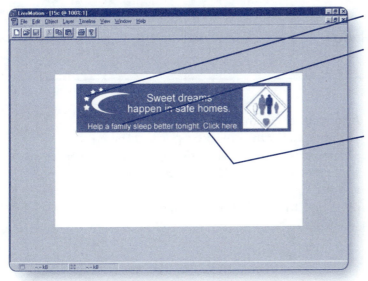

• Stars appear one by one.

• Action line fades in gradually at end of animation.

• Entire graphic animation loops every 8 seconds.

To set the duration for each of the objects in this animation,

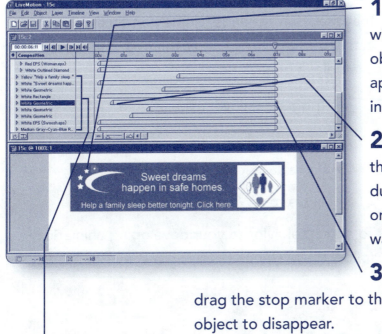

1. In the composition window, click on the first object that you want to appear—the object header in the Timeline highlights.

2. In the Timeline, drag the start marker on the duration bar to the place on the Timeline where you want the object to appear.

3. For the same object, drag the stop marker to the point you want the object to disappear.

4. Continue setting the duration for individual

objects by selecting them in the composition window and indicating their timing in the Timeline.

NOTE

After you specify the duration for individual objects, you need to set the object properties. This is accomplished using keyframes, as covered in Chapter 14, "Working with the LiveMotion Timeline." After you add the keyframes, remember to save your changes by pressing Ctrl+S (Windows users) or Cmd+S (Mac uers).

Adding a Behavior

Behaviors are different from object properties in that they don't change the way an object looks or acts, but they change what the object triggers. For example, a behavior might

- Trigger a rollover event.

- Stop the animation.

- Run a JavaScript.

- Move to a Web page.

To add a behavior to your developing animation, follow these steps:

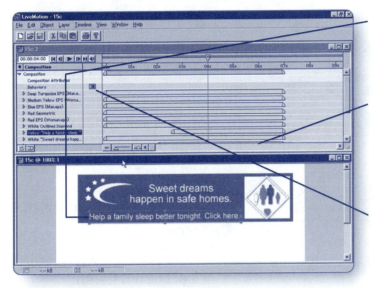

1. Select the object to which you want to assign the behavior.

2. Move the current time marker to the point on the Timeline where you want to add the event.

3. Click on the Behaviors button in the Timeline. The Add Behavior dialog box opens.

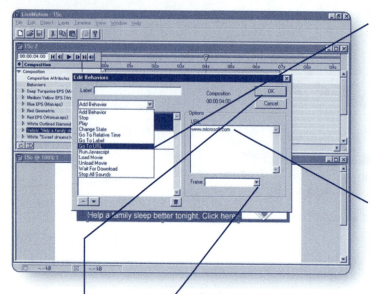

4. Click on the behavior you want to add. (In this example, I chose Go to URL.) Another set of options will appear, depending on the option you select.

5. Type the URL to which you want to link the behavior. If you have selected a different behavior type, a different set of options will appear here.

6. Choose the type of HTML frame you want to use.

TIP

If you plan to use a number of behaviors in your animation, type a name for the behavior in the Label text box. This enables you to apply a label by name in the future rather than having to scroll through the behaviors list to select the one you need.

7. Click on OK to return to the Timeline.

Editing Behaviors

You can edit a behavior from either the Timeline window or selected palettes in the composition window.

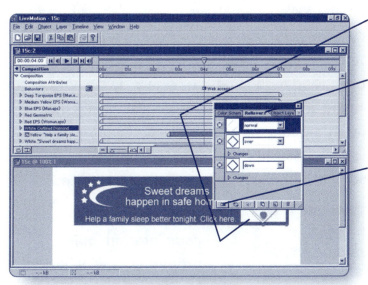

1. Select the object with which you want to work.

2. Open a palette (in this example, Rollovers is selected).

3. Click on the Edit Behaviors button.

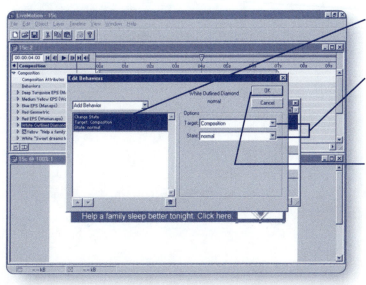

4. Select the behavior you want to modify.

5. Modify the option settings, as necessary, that apply to the selection.

6. Click on OK to return to the composition window.

Creating a Looping Animation

As mentioned earlier in this chapter, adding motion to your Web sites can capture the attention of your visitors and even hold their interest. But you don't want your Web animations to hold visitors hostage as they wait for your files to download. One way you can keep your file size down and still benefit from having motion on the page is by creating a looping animation. A loop does just what it sounds like—it repeats the animation continuously while the composition is displayed (or until you specify an end point). To create a loop, follow these steps:

1. Create your animation, complete with object properties, any behaviors, and sound.

2. Test your animation by pressing the spacebar (Windows or Mac) or by clicking on Play.

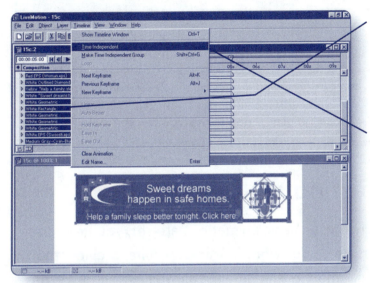

3. Select all of the objects in the Timeline. The object headers will be highlighted.

4. From the Timeline menu, choose Time Independent. A small icon appears to the left of each object header.

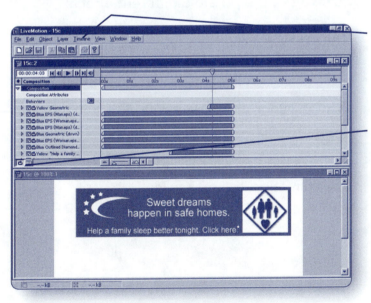

5. From the Timeline menu, choose Loop.

OR

6. Click on the Loop button that appears in the lower-left corner of the Timeline window. The Loop icon is positioned in the object header so that you can see the Loop effect has been applied.

> **TIP**
>
> If you test your looping animation and it doesn't work correctly, check to be sure that all objects *and* the composition header have been selected and looped. If the composition header does not have a loop icon, choose Timeline, Loop to assign one.

Testing Your Animation

Once your basic animations are set, you need to preview your work. For best results, preview the animation in the Timeline as well as in your Web browser to see the possible different effects.

You can preview your work three different ways:

- In the composition window, click on Preview.

- Choose File, Preview In, and the name of your Web browser.

- Press the spacebar (Windows or Mac) to play the animation in the Timeline.

Your animation should play as specified, with any behaviors you added in place. To see the size of your animation file and the amount of time it will require to download to commonly-used systems, click on Export Report.

TIP

Test your animation in as many different browsers as possible before you prepare your file for the Web.

A Quick Summary

This chapter has introduced you to additional techniques you'll use as you create animations in LiveMotion. Whether you are creating a banner ad, a swirling logo, a fading photograph, or a cartoon character that pirouettes across the page, you'll find the process in LiveMotion a fairly simple one. The examples in these two chapters on animation have given you a starting point—but the fun begins when you start to see your own characters and creations come to life.

The next chapter adds a new dimension by exploring the addition of sound to your LiveMotion compositions.

16

Sounding Off with Sound Objects

Rollover effects and animation files are two of the main visual strengths of LiveMotion, but there's another sensory possibility as well: sound. LiveMotion enables you to add sound effects (clangs, beeps, whirrs, and whistles), music, or voice-overs to your compositions. This chapter shows you how to work with sound in your creations. Specifically, you will learn how to:

- Plan how you'll use sound.
- Attach a sound file to an object.
- Add a sound from the Sounds palette.
- Create your own sound files.
- Attach sound to animations.

Planning Your Sound Use

The use of sound is most effective when you follow the "moderation" mindset. Hearing sound should be a pleasing, amusing, interesting, or helpful experience for your visitor—you don't want to inundate a visitor with sound or tie up his or her modem while a large sound file is downloading.

The use of sound can do a number of things in a well-thought-out composition:

- Emphasize an action, like a mouse click or a menu selection.

- Engage a visitor's imagination.

- Provide a "welcome" to the site.

- Reinforce a known brand theme.

- Lead a visitor to the next step on a site.

- Provide a "mood" for browsing that is compatible with the site content.

As you plan how you will use sound in your LiveMotion composition, it is helpful to know that you can add a sound three different ways. You can:

- Create a sound effect for an object action.

- Add a sound object to play at a particular place in an animation.

- Play a music thread in the background as your page is being displayed.

> **NOTE**
>
> Be forewarned, however: Some people dislike hearing "cheesy" background music when they land on a site, so think carefully about the music you add and choose with care. Avoid adding music just because you can and make sure it adds to the visitor's experience of your site.

> **NOTE**
>
> Music files can make your Web downloads fat and cumbersome. Because users won't wait around forever for your music to load, remember to keep an eye on file size and use looping whenever possible.

Here are some ideas for simple ways that sound can be used:

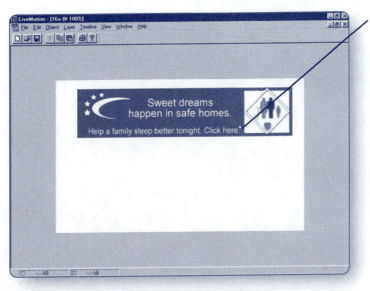

• When the little star appears, a chime sounds, drawing visitors' attention to the fact that the link can be clicked to lead to the sponsor's site.

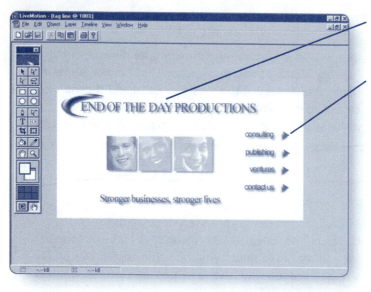

• Simple piano melody plays throughout.

• A "click" is played when the user clicks a button.

Finding Sound Files

Where can you get music files? A number of sites are available on the Web that enable you to download free music clips. One site, http://www.killermusic.com, is partnering with Adobe to provide sound files for use in tutorials hosted online.

Attaching a Sound File to an Object

One of the easiest ways to add sound is to assign a sound event to a rollover. You might use this technique in these instances:

• Add a "ding" or "click" noise when a user clicks a button.

- Add a "stretching" sound as the display changes from one page to another.

- Play a chime when the file has finished downloading.

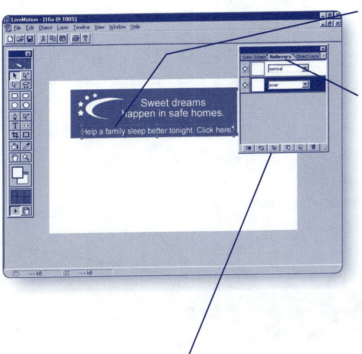

1. Click on the object to which you want to apply the rollover.

2. Open the Rollover palette by pressing F11. Choose the rollover effect you want to use.

> ### NOTE
>
> If you want the sound to begin playing as soon as the user positions the mouse pointer over the object, choose Over. If you want the music to begin when the user clicks on the object, choose Down.

3. Click on the Sounds button in the Rollover palette.

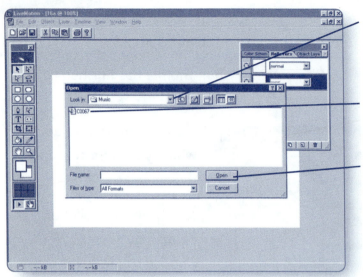

4. Navigate to the folder where you store your sound files.

5. Click on the filename to select it.

6. Click on Open. The sound file is added to the rollover effect.

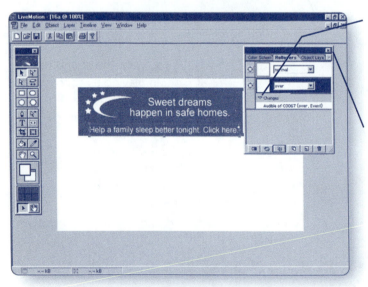

7. Review the addition of the sound file by clicking on the Changes drop-down arrow.

8. Close the Rollover palette.

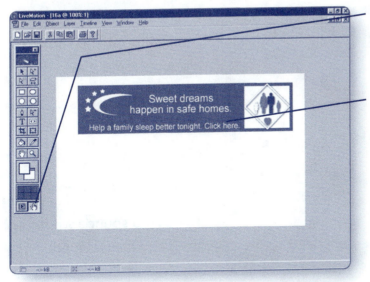

9. Click on the Preview Mode button to test the sound file.

10. Move the pointer to the object with the sound event and test the play.

Adding Sounds from the Sounds Palette

You can also add sounds from the Sounds palette to your LiveMotion compositions. You can assign a sound to the page transition—that is, the sound plays when the page appears—or you can attach a sound to a particular event, or keyframe.

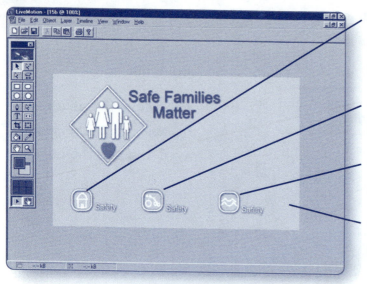

• When the user clicks House Safety, the sound of a door closing plays.

• Bike Safety plays a bicycle bell sound.

• Water Safety plays the sound of water drops.

• A chime sounds when the page is displayed.

Assigning a Sound to the Page Transition

This is a common effect used in many multimedia presentations: As part of the transition from one page to another, a sound is played to lead the viewer's attention. You can easily add a sound to the beginning display of your page. Here are the steps:

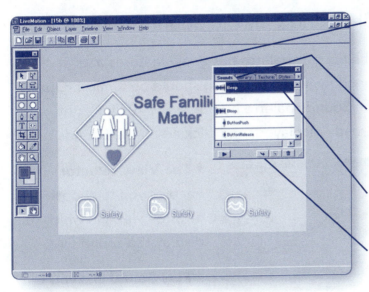

1. Open the composition to which you want to add sound.

2. Open the Sounds palette choosing Window, Sounds.

3. Click on a sound you want to use.

4. Click on the Apply Sound button. The sound is added to the composition.

TIP

You can listen to a selected sound while the Sounds palette is open. Simply double-click the sound or select the sound and click Play.

NOTE

You won't see any visible change in your page—there's nothing obvious to tell you that a sound has just been added. To test the page, click on the Preview Mode button. You also can see where LiveMotion inserted the sound event by displaying the Timeline (press Ctrl+T in Windows or Cmd+T on the Mac).

Checking Out the Sounds Palette

The Sounds palette has a few features and functions with which you should be familiar. Open the Sounds palette by pressing F10 (if it's not already displayed) and clicking on the Sounds tab.

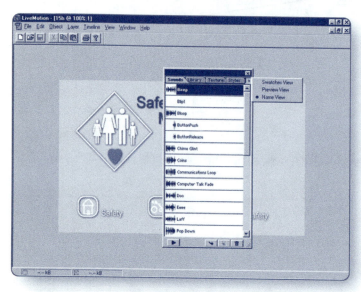

- **The View selector** enables you to choose one of three views in which to display the sound files.

- **Play Sound** lets you preview the sound before you apply it to your composition or object.

- **Apply Sound** applies the selected sound to the composition or object.

- **New Sound** opens a dialog box so that you can enter a new name for a sound being added to the palette.

- **Delete Sound** removes the selected sound from the palette.

Changing the View in the Sounds Palette

The Sounds palette gives you a choice of three different ways to view the sounds stored there. The

Name view, shown by default, provides the name of the file and a small thumbnail of each file. Additionally, you can choose these views:

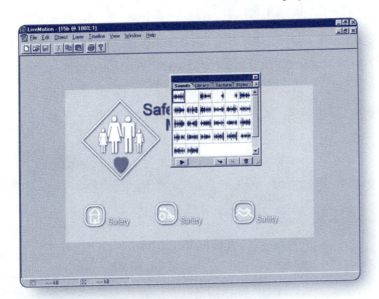

- **Swatches View** displays a sounds-only view of the sound choices.

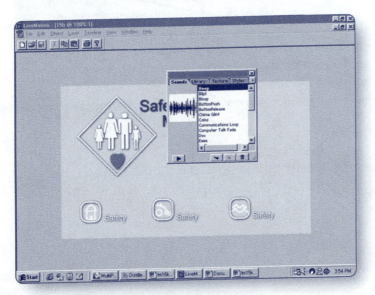

- **Preview View** provides the name of the sound file and displays a larger view of the sound itself.

Creating Your Own Sound Files

You can easily add a voice—your own if you like—to your site by using the recording feature built into your Macintosh or PC. Windows systems come with the Sound Recorder utility built in, and the Mac, likewise, has a recording feature. These features allow you to easily add a quick voice-over or miscellaneous sound effect (a cat's meow, a door closing, a bell ringing ... you get the idea).

> **NOTE**
>
> For truly professional sound, however, you'll want to use a digital recording device, especially if you are relying on the spoken word and its carrying capability. Clarity is the name of the game for high-quality sound recordings. But beware—sound files get *huge*, so look for opportunities to keep the files short and loop them, or find compressed files on the Web as opposed to using "roll-your-own" sounds.

The simple steps for recording your sound (this example is based on a Windows system) are:

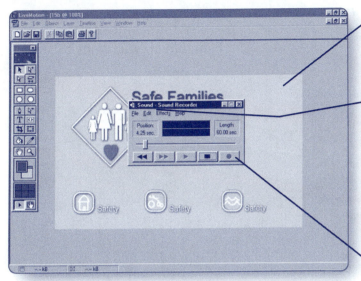

1. Make sure your microphone is attached and working properly.

2. Open the Sound Recorder by choosing Start, Programs, Accessories, Entertainment, Sound Recorder.

3. Click on the Record button and record your sound.

TIP

Be sure to use Rewind and Play to listen to your sound before saving it. If you need to re-record your sound, simply click on the Record button and repeat the steps.

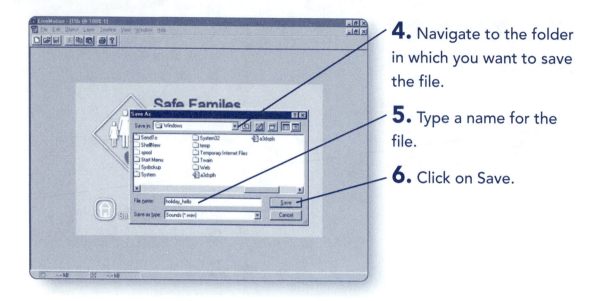

4. Navigate to the folder in which you want to save the file.

5. Type a name for the file.

6. Click on Save.

Attaching Sound to Animations

You've learned to add a sound file to an object by using the Rollover palette, and you've found out how to apply a music file to your overall composition. You can also add sounds to your animations, either by placing them directly in the Timeline or by adding a specific sound at an event or keyframe.

Adding Sound to the Composition

When you want to add a sound file to your composition, whether you are using a voice-over introduction, a piece of music, or a sound effect,

you can use the Place command to add the file.
Here are the steps:

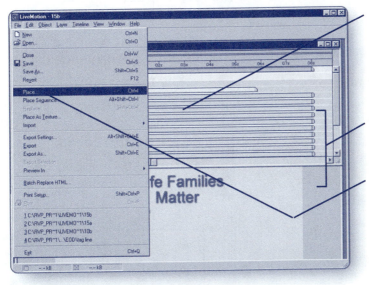

1. Open the Timeline window by pressing Ctrl+T (Windows users) or Cmd+T (Mac users).

2. Tile the display by choosing Window, Tile.

3. From the File menu, choose Place. The Place dialog box opens.

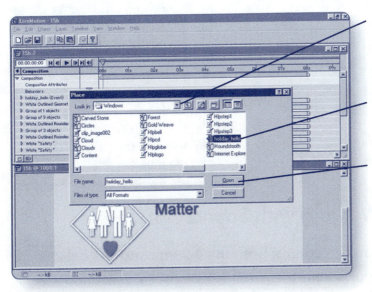

4. Navigate to the folder where the sound file is stored.

5. Select the file. The file is highlighted.

6. Click on Open. The file is added to the composition.

Sound Files in the Timeline

As soon as you add the file, it appears in the Timeline.

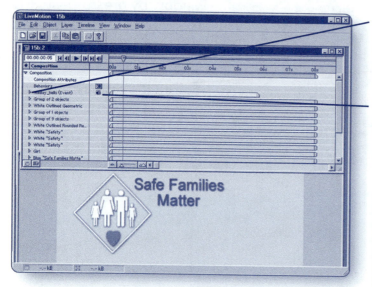

• Sound file appears just below the composition header.

• Click on the Sound button to turn sound on and off.

TIP

After you add a sound to your composition, you can also add it to the Sounds palette. From the Timeline, click on the sound object header to select it; then drag it to the Sounds palette. A Name dialog box opens so that you can name the file; click on OK. The sound is then added to the palette.

Working with Sound Options

You can control both the volume and the balance of your sound files from within your LiveMotion composition.

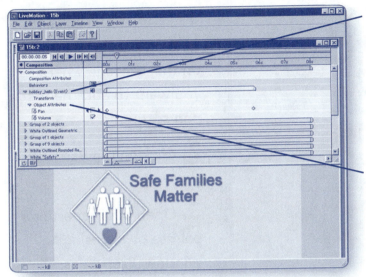

1. Click on the sound file's drop-down arrow to display object properties. The Transform and Object Attributes categories appear.

2. Click on Object Attributes. You see the Pan and Volume sound properties.

Controlling Pan

The pan property controls the balance of sound from a dual-speaker system. You might want to shift the sound from one side to another, to give the visitor the feeling of movement (like an airplane passing overhead), or distribute it equally, like you would set the best sound balance on a set of traditional stereo speakers. Here are the steps for setting the pan value:

1. Position the current time marker at the point on the Timeline where you want to add the first pan setting.

2. Click on the Pan stopwatch.

3. Open the Properties palette by choosing Window, Properties.

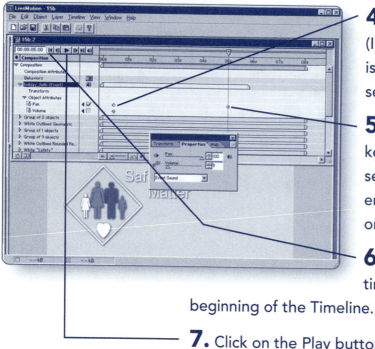

4. Set the first keyframe. (In this example, the value is set to the leftmost setting.)

5. Set the second keyframe. This example sets the keyframe at the end of the sound object, on the rightmost setting.

6. Rewind the current time marker to the beginning of the Timeline.

7. Click on the Play button to preview. (For the

example shown here, the sound coming from the speakers "moves" from left to right.)

Working with Volume

Volume is nothing mysterious—you control the overall volume and changes in the volume level by setting keyframes to handle the events. You might want to fade out a piece of music, for example, or have music get softer when the visitor clicks a certain object. To change the volume of your composition,

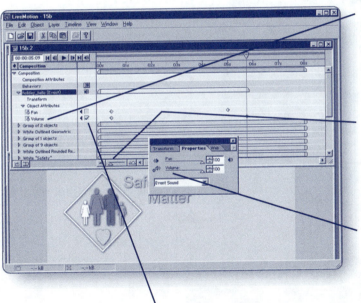

1. Click on the Volume stopwatch. The Add/Remove keyframe check box appears.

2. Drag the current time marker to the place you want to set the first keyframe.

3. Set the Volume settings the way you want them.

4. Click on the check box to add a keyframe at the current time marker position. Continue adding keyframes if you want to vary the sound level during animation.

Specify a Solo Sound Event

In the event that you have multiple sound files going at once on your page, you may want to make sure a certain sound file gets played without any overlap from other objects. For example, if you create a rollover that plays your brand song, you can override any blips and beeps that might come from other events on your composition. To do this, you specify a sound as a "solo" event. Here's how:

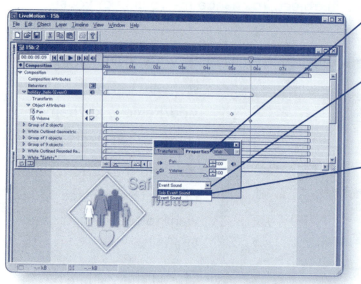

1. Open the Properties palette by pressing F8.

2. In the Properties palette, click on the Event Sound drop-down arrow.

3. Select Solo Event Sound. This protects the sound object so that it is the only sound playing at a given time.

A Quick Summary

In this chapter, you learned how to add more life to your compositions by adding sound. A sound can be as simple as a beep or as complex as classical music. You can read poetry or do your favorite QuickDraw McGraw impression. But be forewarned—sound files get very large very quickly, and you don't want to keep your visitors waiting. Optimize your use of sound to add special touches to your compositions, but keep them as lean as possible. The next chapter takes you closer to the Web by helping you establish links to files and URLs in your LiveMotion compositions.

17

Linking Objects

The last few chapters have focused on ways you can make your LiveMotion compositions interactive by adding rollovers and animations. The technique in this chapter takes the viewers of your site to a new place, by linking them to other pages on the Web or providing access to files. Specifically, in this chapter, you will learn how to

- Work with the Web palette.
- Link to a Web page.
- Replace Web text with graphics.
- Divide an image into several links.

Working with the Web Palette

The Web palette is the place where you'll identify the pages and/or files to which you want to link your LiveMotion objects. Before you begin establishing the links, complete your composition and test any rollover or animation feature you've added.

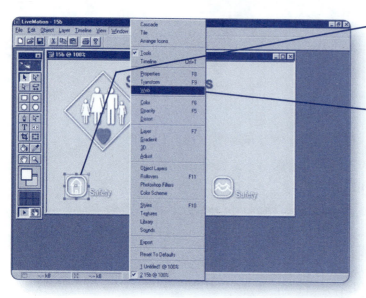

1. Select the object for which you want to create the link.

2. From the Window menu, choose Web. The Web palette opens.

The Web palette enables you to link your objects to a Web address or a file.

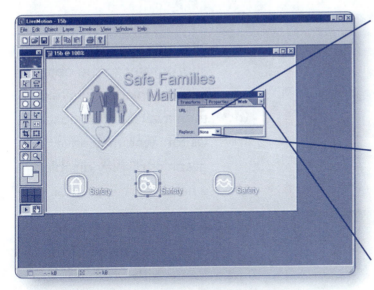

• The Web page link box, URL, gives you the space to type the Web page address for the page to which you want to link.

• Replace options enable you to replace text with graphics objects you create in LiveMotion.

• View selector gives you an alternate way to display the Web palette selections. Click on the arrow to view display choices and to make your selection from the shortcut menu that appears.

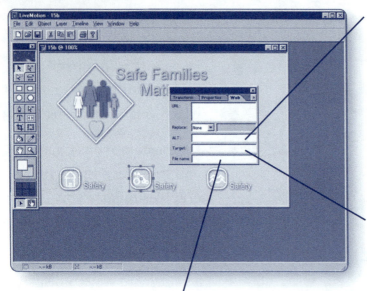

• ALT provides you with an alternate way to name and/or refer to the object you are linking. This text is then available for those visitors who may have graphics display disabled when they access your site.

• Target allows you to specify the name of the frame with which you are working, if your page uses frames, and to open another browser window, if you choose.

• File name is the name that is assigned to the object when you export it to HTML.

Linking to a Web Page

When you're ready to establish a link between the object you've created and a Web page, you can do so by clicking on a live Web page or a page on your computer or server. Here are the steps:

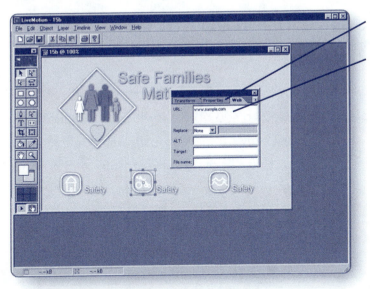

1. Open the Web palette.

2. Click in the URL text box and type the Web address to which you want to link.

NOTE

If you are linking to a page on the Web, be sure to include the entire page address, such as http://www.sample.com.

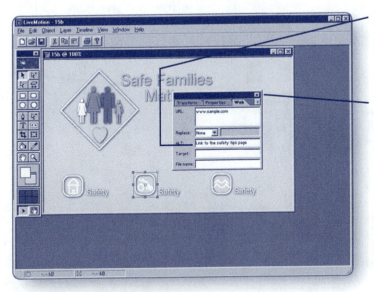

3. Click in the ALT text box and type descriptive text about the link.

4. Click on the Close box to close the Web palette.

TIP

If you preview your page, don't be concerned when your link doesn't work. That process is taken care of when you export the file, which is discussed in Chapter 18, "Exporting LiveMotion Creations."

Replacing Web Text with Graphics

If you've been creating simple text pages with HTML, you'll be pleased to see how easy it is to replace plain text with your LiveMotion compositions. You can strip out a standard text heading, for example, and slide in a slick, styled, company logo or title for your site.

Here are the steps:

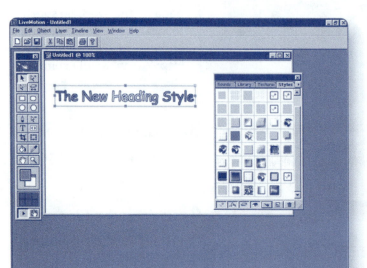

1. Select the object you want to use.

2. Set the style, color, and shadow for the object, then save the object.

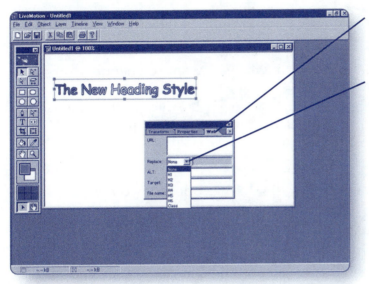

3. Open the Web palette by choosing Window, Web.

4. Click on the Replace drop-down arrow. A list of choices appears. Click on the item you want to replace.

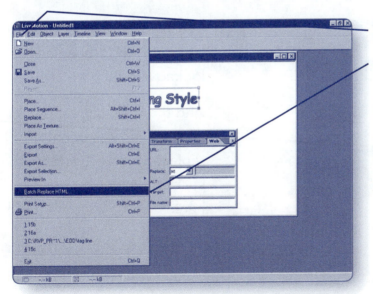

5. Open the File menu.

6. Choose Batch Replace HTML. The Open dialog box will open so that you can choose the HTML file that contains the headings you want to replace.

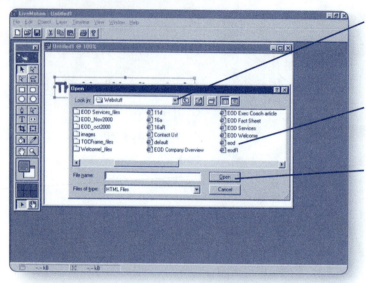

7. Navigate to the folder containing the file you want to change.

8. Click on the file name to select it.

9. Click on Open. The file opens in your Web browser.

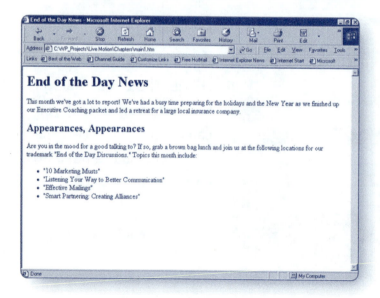

The Web page with the standard <H1> heading looked like this:

And the Web page after the heading has been replaced with a LiveMotion stylized heading appears here:

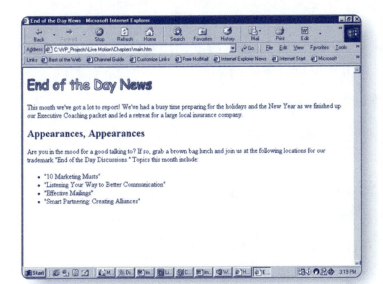

NOTE

You can replace six different heading styles automatically in LiveMotion. This is a great feature for making sure you have a consistent style and treatment for multiple Web pages or for a multi-page site.

Dividing an Image into Several Links

Image mapping is the process by which you divide a single graphic into regions that are linked to other pages or files on your computer, server, or on the Web. You might use an image map to do the following:

- Invite a visitor to explore different rooms in a building.

- Enable a visitor to select different meals on a visual menu.

- Use the photo of a class to provide links to individual Web pages.

Creating an image map is really a simple process of dividing a single image or photo into a number of different links. Here's how:

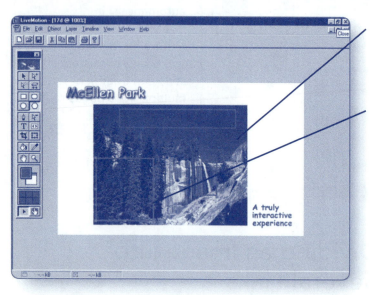

1. Start by placing or creating the photo or image you want to use.

2. Add shapes to identify the places where you want to add the links.

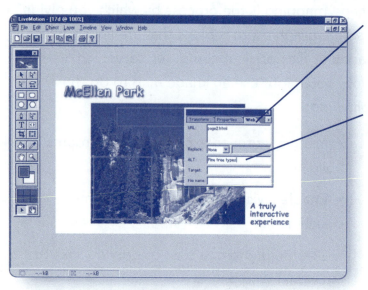

3. Use the Web palette to add links to the shapes you have added.

4. Enter descriptors, as needed, in the ALT text box.

> **TIP**
>
> Make sure your image map is clear for your readers. If you don't include a visible boundary box, use text or a rollover note to highlight the areas of the map that are linked. This will help your visitors navigate through your site more easily.

A Quick Summary

This chapter has provided the steps for doing some Web work with LiveMotion. Specifically, you learned how to link your compositions to Web pages and files, batch replace old HTML headings with your new LiveMotion objects, and create image maps you can use in the sites you create. The next step, and the subject of the next chapter, involves exporting your LiveMotion creations into formats you can use on the Web and in other programs.

18

Exporting LiveMotion Creations

Throughout this book, you've learned how to create LiveMotion compositions that enable you to add style, color, special 3D effects, animations, sound, and other special effects to your creations. Now you're ready for one of the final steps: Turning your LiveMotion compositions into files you can use on the Web and in other programs. Specifically, in this chapter, you'll learn to

- Export entire compositions.
- Export selected objects.
- Choose export options.
- Finish the export.

> **TIP**
>
> You can enter your export settings two different ways: By displaying the Export palette (choose Export from the Window menu) or, alternatively, from the File menu, choose Export Settings (Alt+Shift+Ctrl+E in Windows or Opt+Shift+Cmd+E on the Mac).

Exporting Entire Compositions

As you know, LiveMotion gives you the means to create entire Web pages, full graphic layouts, or animations and special effects that are complete compositions in themselves. You can easily export your LiveMotion creation to formats that make them usable in other programs and on the Web. To begin the process of exporting a composition:

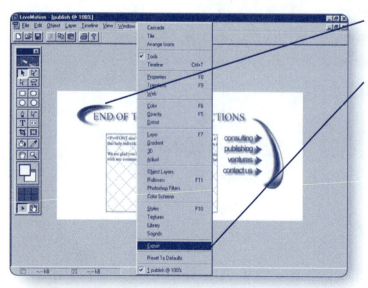

1. Open the composition you want to export.

2. Choose Window, Export. The Export palette opens.

Checking Out the Export Palette

The Export palette contains most of the settings you need to export both entire compositions and selected objects. Here are the important elements in the Export palette:

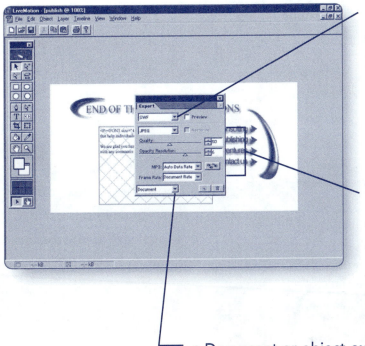

• The Export format you choose depends on how you want to use the exported file. You can choose SWF (Flash), Photoshop, GIF, JPEG, and two kinds of PNG format.

• Optimization settings vary from format to format. These items enable you to choose the graphics and sound quality of the file you export.

• Document or object export selection enables you to choose whether you want to export the entire document or only the selected objects.

Understanding Format Choices

The following screens show you the various optimization settings for each of the format choices:

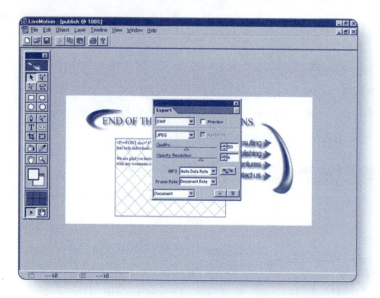

• SWF (Flash format) enables you to choose the quality, opacity, audio format, and frame rate.

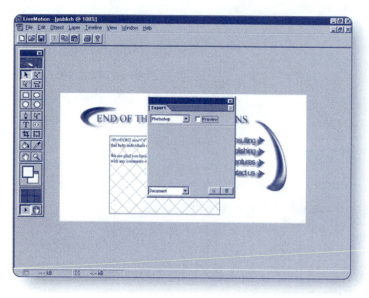

• Photoshop gives you the option of saving the composition in Photoshop format.

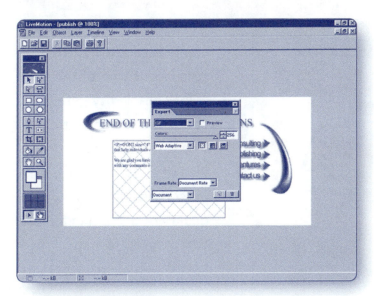

• GIF lets you export your compositions in a common format for the Web. GIF is a fairly simple format, without a great number of colors or varying opacity. GIF is a good choice when it's important to keep file size down and choose a format supported by virtually all browsers.

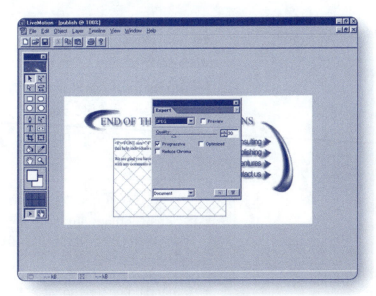

• JPEG is also used for exporting compositions for the Web. This format supports a greater number of shading and color changes than the GIF format. Use JPEG when you have a detailed photo or image and want to show all the subtleties.

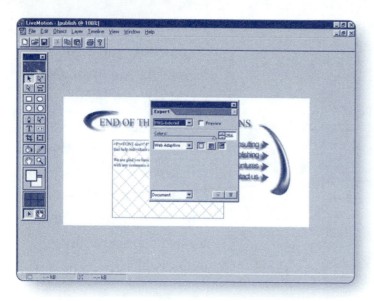

• PNG-Indexed provides a compressed format that strips out some of the color complexity in favor of a smaller, tighter file. This format is good for files of all types and preserved the higher quality of a JPEG in a more compressed format.

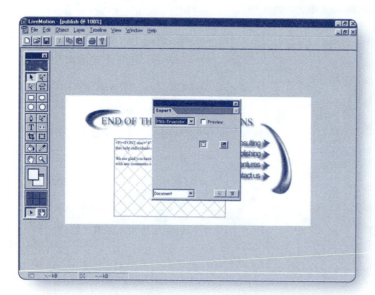

• PNG-Truecolor creates a Web format that uses the full breadth of color but compresses the file size to manageable proportions.

NOTE

Different settings are available for each of the different file formats in the Export palette. Depending on the format in which you want to export the file, you will see different options from those shown here.

Preparing to Export Selected Objects

The process of exporting a selected object is simply a matter of choosing the objects you want to export and making a few choices. LiveMotion uses a process called slicing to select only the objects you want when you export specific objects instead of an entire composition. Here are the steps for preparing to export selected objects:

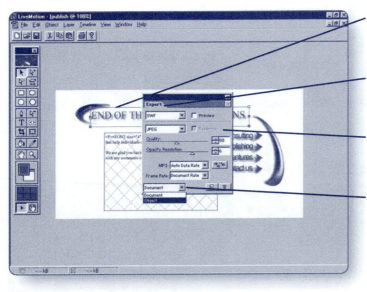

1. Select the object you want to export.

2. Open the Export palette.

3. Set optimization options.

4. Click on the selection drop-down arrow. If you want to export the selected object, click on Object.

TIP

Always keep a copy of the objects you create in their native LiveMotion format. If you choose, you can also add objects to the Library palette so that you can use them again easily.

Going Back to Composition Settings

The next step in exporting your file involves checking—and perhaps changing—the Export settings you selected in the Composition window. You first saw the Composition window when you created a new LiveMotion file; the Composition Settings dialog box opens by default. Start by getting back to that box:

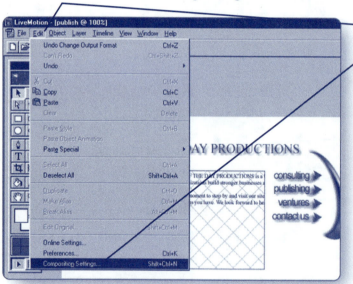

1. Open the Edit menu.

2. Select Composition Settings. The Composition Settings dialog box opens.

TIP

Display the Composition Settings dialog box quickly by pressing Shift+Ctrl+N (Windows users) or Shift+Cmd+N (Mac users).

3. Click on the Export drop-down arrow. A list of choices appears so that you can make your selection. Here's a quick description of what these selections do:

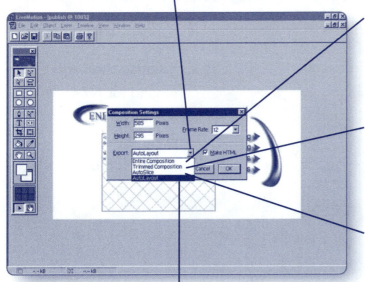

• **Entire Composition** gathers up your entire composition and exports it in the format you choose.

• **Trimmed Composition** "slices" out the objects you have selected and exports only those items.

• **AutoSlice** divides each object or group into separate files and exports the objects individually. An HTML page is created that provides the links for the sliced objects.

• **AutoLayout** divides the composition but keeps the full composition together in the HTML page that is created (unlike AutoSlice, which separates the objects and uses the HTML page to refer to the objects).

NOTE

Both Entire Composition and Trimmed Composition give you the option of choosing whether to create an HTML file during the export process. If your goal is to create an image, leave HTML unselected.

TIP

AutoLayout and AutoSlice automatically generate HTML files; you are given the option with Entire Composition and Trimmed Composition to save as HTML.

Finishing the Export

The last step in exporting your LiveMotion composition (or selection) actually exports the file in the new format you have chosen. Here are the steps:

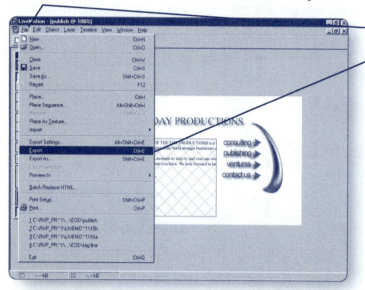

1. Open the File menu.

2. Choose the Export command (or press Ctrl+E for Windows users or Cmd+E for Mac users). The Export dialog box opens.

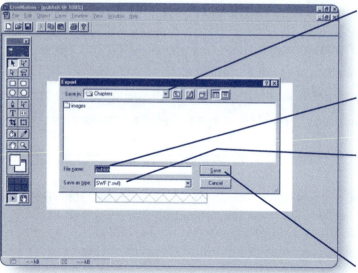

3. Navigate to the folder in which you want to save the exported file.

4. Type a file name for the new file.

5. Make sure the Save as Type setting reflects your selection in the Export palette.

6. Click on Save. The file is exported as you specified.

> **NOTE**
>
> To export only the current selection, be sure to select the objects before you choose Export. When you select the objects, the Export Selection command in the File menu becomes available.

A Quick Summary

This chapter has spotlighted the procedures you will use to make your LiveMotion compositions usable in other programs. The next chapter wraps up this book by providing information on how you can use LiveMotion with other Adobe products.

19

Integrating LiveMotion with Other Adobe Products

If LiveMotion is the first Adobe product you've worked with, you will be pleased to discover that you have a full berth of Web-generation programs at your disposal. This chapter introduces you to some of the integration possibilities available in LiveMotion. Specifically, you will learn to

- Work with Photoshop filters.
- Use Photoshop files.
- Prepare LiveMotion compositions for Adobe GoLive.

A Full Complement of Web Tools

Adobe publishes a complete Web collection that mixes and matches the talents of four different programs. LiveMotion is the Web animation and graphics offering, but that's just one part of a full system. If you want to fully complement your Web experience, you can also use the following programs:

- Adobe GoLive, an easy-to-use yet powerful Web page generation program.

- Adobe Photoshop, a powerful photo and bitmap graphics editor.

- Adobe Illustrator, the standard vector-graphics program.

What this means to you is that you can create original art in Illustrator or Photoshop, bring the art into LiveMotion to stylize and animate it, and then export it to use in the full-featured, integrated Web site you create with GoLive.

TIP

GoLive, Photoshop, and Illustrator are all able to open and read files created in LiveMotion.

> **NOTE**
>
> For ideas, offers, and free trials of some Adobe Web products, visit Adobe online at http://www.adobe.com. You can also move directly to the Adobe site by establishing your Internet connection and clicking the topmost section of the Tools palette.

Working with Photoshop Filters

With the idea of making shifting between Photoshop and LiveMotion as seamless for users as possible, Adobe packaged a number of Photoshop filters with LiveMotion. Using the Photoshop filters, you can alter objects, colors, patterns, and text to get an almost unlimited array of effects.

> **NOTE**
>
> Filters work with bitmapped graphics only—the process modifies the pixels used to make up the image. The best filtering effects appear when there is some variance in the image before you begin; in other words, a solid-blue object won't show much difference when you apply a filter, but a graded image or a multi-color photo will show the change the filter brings.

Applying Filters from the Objects Menu

The Photoshop filters available in LiveMotion are housed in the Objects menu. You will find not only a wide range of different filter types, but an almost infinite number of ways in which you can customize the look you want. Here are the steps for applying a Photoshop filter to an object:

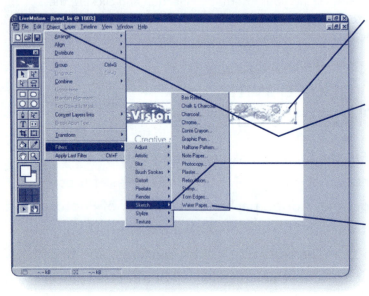

1. Select the object to which you want to apply the filter.

2. From the Objects menu, choose Filters.

3. Choose the filter type you want to use.

4. Select the specific filter you want to apply.

Each individual filter opens its own dialog box.

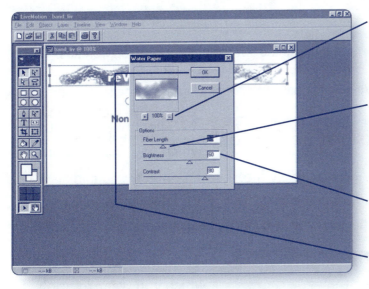

5. Click on the + or – buttons to adjust the display.

6a. Use the sliders to adjust filter settings.

OR

6b. Type the value for the setting you want to use

7. Click on OK to save the settings and update the selected object.

TIP

If you like the effect you've created after you've chosen your filter settings, save the object settings to the Styles palette for later use.

Understanding Filters

- Filters work only with bitmapped images.
- Filters must be applied to entire objects; not layers.
- You can create a new filter effect by mixing two filters and adding them to the Styles palette.

TIP
You can reuse the last filter with which you worked by choosing Object, Apply Last Filter.

Using the Photoshop Filters Palette

Once you apply filters to an object, you can suppress the display and/or remove filters by working with the Photoshop Filters palette.

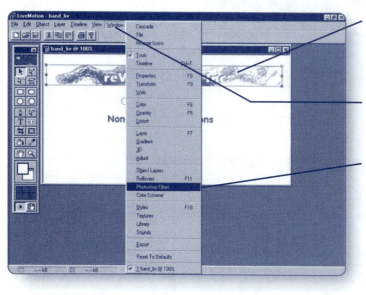

1. Select the object to which you want to apply the filter.

2. Open the Window menu.

3. Choose Photoshop Filters. The Photoshop Filters palette opens.

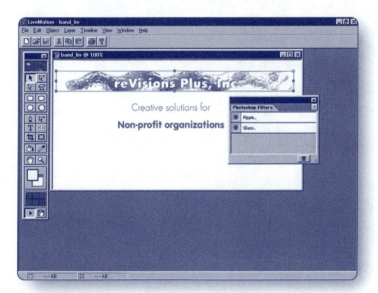

• The filters are shown in the list area. The highlighted filter is the currently selected filter.

• Show/Hide selector enables you to suppress the effect of a particular filter.

• Delete Filter removes the selected filter.

TIP

You can move easily to the settings for a specific filter by double-clicking the filter. The settings dialog box for that filter type will open. You can then make your changes and click on OK; the selected object will be updated.

Using Photoshop Files

Earlier in the book, in Chapter 5, "Adding and Importing Objects," you learned that you can easily place images you create in Photoshop by simply opening the File menu and choosing the Place command.

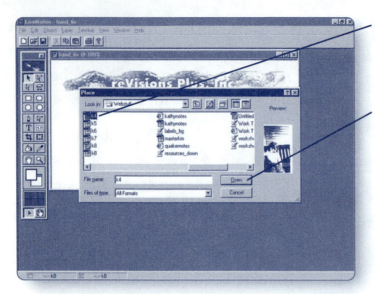

• Photoshop files are highlighted with a special file icon.

• Files can be opened directly into LiveMotion.

NOTE

You can also place a sequence of files to be used in an animation for both Photoshop and Illustrator by choosing the Place Sequence command in the File menu.

Converting Photoshop Layers to Objects

When you import layered Photoshop or Illustrator files, the animation gets a little more challenging. By default, LiveMotion treats Photoshop or Illustrator images as one complete object when imported. You can change the individual layers into objects so that you can animate them independently, if necessary. To convert the original layers in a Photoshop or Illustrator image, follow these steps:

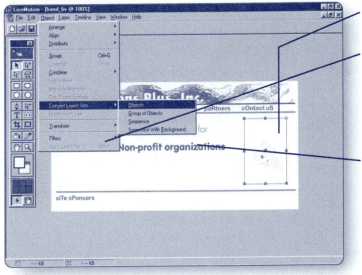

1. Place the object.

2. From the Objects menu, choose Convert Layers Into. A submenu will appear.

3. Click on Objects. The Photoshop layers are then marked as Objects and you can animate each one individually, if you choose.

NOTE

You can edit files you create and import from Adobe Photoshop and Illustrator by selecting the object, opening the Edit menu, and choosing Edit Original. The file will open in its native program. When you make and save your changes you are returned to your LiveMotion composition.

Using LiveMotion Compositions in Adobe GoLive

As you learned in the preceding chapter, you can easily export your LiveMotion compositions—entire compositions or individual objects—in HTML format, usable on the Web and with all Web-generation programs.

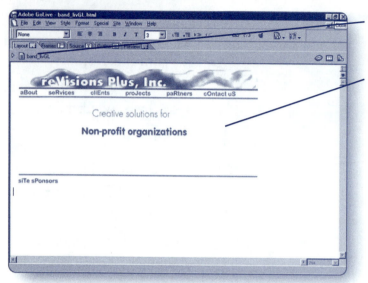

• The LiveMotion file was exported as HTML.

• The file appears in the Layout window of GoLive as it appeared in LiveMotion.

TIP

In the newest version of Adobe GoLive, version 5.0, you can use Smart Links to edit LiveMotion objects directly within GoLive. When you double-click a LiveMotion object in GoLive, LiveMotion is opened and you can make any changes necessary to the object. When you close the application, LiveMotion updates the original file so your changes are preserved in both the original and the image in the GoLive composition.

Viewing HTML in GoLive

You can easily use HTML script generated during the LiveMotion export procedure in HTML editors and other Web generators, including GoLive. In GoLive, you can view the LiveMotion script by clicking the Source tab.

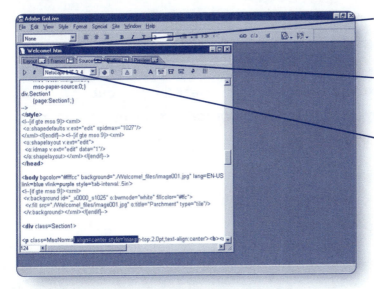

• Name the open LiveMotion export file.

• HTML code is displayed in the Source tab.

• Click on the Layout tab to see the object or page as it appears in LiveMotion.

TIP

You can also view the HTML file created in any text editor of your choosing. If you want to see the HTML file created when you exported your LiveMotion composition, you can open it in word processing program. Be sure to save the file with the same file extension, so GoLive or any other Web page editor will be able to recognize it as an HTML file.

A Quick Summary

This chapter wraps up this book by encouraging you to check into using other Adobe companion products to complement your animation and graphics designs for the Web. You can easily leverage the power and flexibility of LiveMotion animations by using the equally powerful offerings in Photoshop, Illustrator, and GoLive. And no matter how many tools you acquire, remember to explore them often. The best thing about LiveMotion is not the program's talent—it's yours. Enjoy your creations!

Glossary

3D effects. Special effects you can apply to an object or a group of objects that make the items appear to "stand out" from the screen.

A

Active matte. A process that applies a shape as an overlay to another object.

Alignment. Arranging text so that it lines up along a left, right, or center mark.

Alpha channel. The primary input channel for the source.

ALT. A text field in the Web palette that enables you to add a line of alternate text for visitors who do not have images enabled in their view.

Animations. Objects or layers that move or change over a designated time period.

Audio clips. Segments of sound files used as sound effects or background music.

AutoSlice. An export setting in which the selected objects are "sliced" from the composition and saved as an HTML file.

B

Batch replacing. A means of replacing all existing headers or specified code in an HTML script with a LiveMotion object you've created.

Behavior tracks. Lines on the LiveMotion Timeline that enable you to see where events occur over time.

Bevel effect. A 3D effect that makes a button or shape appear to rise off the screen.

C

Compositions. The term used to describe a file created in LiveMotion.

Compression. The process of reducing file size for graphics, audio, and Web files.

Cropping. Reducing the displayed area of an image while keeping the size of the image the same.

Current time marker. Also referred to as the CTM, the current time marker shows the current time selected on the LiveMotion Timeline.

D

Distortion. A special effect applied to LiveMotion graphics that blurs, whirls, or otherwise modifies the selected image.

Duration. The length of time an animation plays.

E

Embossing. A visual treatment that raises and adds a shine effect to an object.

Exporting. Saving a file in a format usable in other programs and on the Web.

F

Filters. Special Photoshop effects that enable you to further modify the bitmapped images you create and import.

Flash. A popular Web animation program. LiveMotion exports files in Flash (swf) format.

Foreground. The color applied to images, text, and shapes placed in the composition.

G

GIF. An acronym for Graphical Interchange Format, GIF files are very common on the Web and are widely supported.

Gradients. A special effect that enables you to fade and shade an image, a shape, or a color.

Grid. A mesh of horizontal and vertical guides that help you create your objects according to linear boundaries. The Grid will not print when you print your LiveMotion compositions.

Guides. Nonprinting lines that appear over your objects as you are working with them, helping you make sure that different parts of your object align in the desired way.

I

Image maps. Adding a number of links to a single graphical object.

J

JPEG. An acronym for Joint Photographic Experts Group, JPEG (jpg) is a popular file format for Web graphics files.

K

Keyframes. An event marker in the LiveMotion Timeline.

L

Layers. Individual slices of objects you can stylize, move, align, and animate as needed.

Links. URLs or file names attached to an image or object that provide a path when the user clicks the object.

Looping. An animation feature that replays an animation segment until interrupted by the user.

M

Mouseovers. Another term for rollover. A mouseover is a type of behavior that occurs when the user positions the mouse pointer over an object.

O

Object-oriented graphics. The type of graphic object that is created in a drawing program. Object-oriented graphics, also called vector images, like those created in Adobe Illustrator, define images through the use of mathematical calculations, which enables them to be redrawn and resized with no loss of clarity.

Offsetting. The process of setting a shadow or image off from another.

Opacity. A setting that enables you to determine whether you want the object to be transparent, solid, or something in-between.

P

Palettes. Small pop-up tool and option sets in LiveMotion. You use the options and buttons in a palette to set the individual specifications for the selected object.

PNG. A graphics file format (Portable Network Graphics) that is available in an indexed and true color format.

Properties. The individual settings related to a selected object.

R

Raster images. Also called a bitmapped graphic, a type of image that is made of a collection of individual dots, or pixels. Unlike a vector image, raster images lose quality when they are enlarged.

Rollovers. A type of animated sequence that causes an action to occur when an object is highlighted by the mouse or clicked on.

S

Styles. Preset characteristics in LiveMotion that enable you to apply a particular look, color, behavior, and shadow to a selected object. The Styles palette provides you with a number of predesigned styles.

T

Textures. Another type of style in LiveMotion that enables you to add a different look to your selected object.

Timeline. A window in LiveMotion where you create, modify, and preview the animations you create.

Trigger object. The object in a remote rollover that triggers a rollover response.

Index

ARE YOU READY FOR A CHANGE?

PRIMA TECH

FOR A CHANGE.

Some publishers create books they think you want. We create books we know you want.
That's because when computer users talk, we listen. Isn't it time for a change? PRIMA TECH.

www.prima-tech.com

PRIMA TECH Is On The Web!

Visit www.prima-tech.com Today

READ about PRIMA TECH'S latest titles.

SEARCH for PRIMA TECH titles by series or category.

SEND your comments on books you've read.

E-MAIL PRIMA TECH'S customer service department.

FIND FAQ's about PRIMA TECH computer books.

RECEIVE technical support for CD's included in PRIMA TECH books.

READ about technical updates to specific titles.

ACCESS a complete listing of PRIMA TECH titles.

Installation Instructions

Browsing the CD-ROM via the CD-ROM Interface

1. Insert the CD-ROM into your CD-ROM drive.

2. From the Windows desktop, double-click the My Computer icon.

3. Double-click the icon representing your CD-ROM drive.

4. Double-click the icon titled start_here.htm to run the interface.

5. The interface works best if viewed using Internet Explorer 4.0 or later.

License Agreement/Notice of Limited Warranty

By opening the sealed disk container in this book, you agree to the following terms and conditions. If, upon reading the following license agreement and notice of limited warranty, you cannot agree to the terms and conditions set forth, return the unused book with unopened disk to the place where you purchased it for a refund.

License:

The enclosed software is copyrighted by the copyright holder(s) indicated on the software disk. You are licensed to copy the software onto a single computer for use by a single concurrent user and to a backup disk. You may not reproduce, make copies, or distribute copies or rent or lease the software in whole or in part, except with written permission of the copyright holder(s). You may transfer the enclosed disk only together with this license, and only if you destroy all other copies of the software and the transferee agrees to the terms of the license. You may not decompile, reverse assemble, or reverse engineer the software.

Notice of Limited Warranty:

The enclosed disk is warranted by Prima Publishing to be free of physical defects in materials and workmanship for a period of sixty (60) days from end user's purchase of the book/disk combination. During the sixty-day term of the limited warranty, Prima will provide a replacement disk upon the return of a defective disk.

Limited Liability:

THE SOLE REMEDY FOR BREACH OF THIS LIMITED WARRANTY SHALL CONSIST ENTIRELY OF REPLACEMENT OF THE DEFECTIVE DISK. IN NO EVENT SHALL PRIMA OR THE AUTHORS BE LIABLE FOR ANY OTHER DAMAGES, INCLUDING LOSS OR CORRUPTION OF DATA, CHANGES IN THE FUNCTIONAL CHARACTERISTICS OF THE HARDWARE OR OPERATING SYSTEM, DELETERIOUS INTERACTION WITH OTHER SOFTWARE, OR ANY OTHER SPECIAL, INCIDENTAL, OR CONSEQUENTIAL DAMAGES THAT MAY ARISE, EVEN IF PRIMA AND/OR THE AUTHOR HAVE PREVIOUSLY BEEN NOTIFIED THAT THE POSSIBILITY OF SUCH DAMAGES EXISTS.

Disclaimer of Warranties:

PRIMA AND THE AUTHORS SPECIFICALLY DISCLAIM ANY AND ALL OTHER WARRANTIES, EITHER EXPRESS OR IMPLIED, INCLUDING WARRANTIES OF MERCHANTABILITY, SUITABILITY TO A PARTICULAR TASK OR PURPOSE, OR FREEDOM FROM ERRORS. SOME STATES DO NOT ALLOW FOR EXCLUSION OF IMPLIED WARRANTIES OR LIMITATION OF INCIDENTAL OR CONSEQUENTIAL DAMAGES, SO THESE LIMITATIONS MAY NOT APPLY TO YOU.

Other:

This Agreement is governed by the laws of the State of California without regard to choice of law principles. The United Convention of Contracts for the International Sale of Goods is specifically disclaimed. This Agreement constitutes the entire agreement between you and Prima Publishing regarding use of the software.